Presented To:

Jeremy Maier

By:

Keith Jandura

Date:

Mar. 29/09

TRUTH UNPLUGGED

**Stories for Guys on Faith, Love,
and Things That Matter Most**

HONOR ⒽⒷ BOOKS
FROM DAVID C. COOK

TRUTH UNPLUGGED–
STORIES FOR GUYS ON FAITH, LOVE, AND THINGS THAT MATTER MOST
Published by Honor Books®, an imprint of
David C. Cook
4050 Lee Vance View
Colorado Springs, CO 80918 U.S.A.

David C. Cook Distribution Canada
55 Woodslee Avenue, Paris, Ontario, Canada N3L 3E5

David C. Cook U.K., Kingsway Communications
Eastbourne, East Sussex BN23 6NT, England

David C. Cook and the graphic circle C logo
are registered trademarks of Cook Communications Ministries.

Unless otherwise noted, Scripture quotations are taken from the *Holy Bible, New International Version*®. NIV®. Copyright © 1973, 1978, 1984 by International Bible Society. Used by permission of Zondervan. All rights reserved. Scripture quotations marked NKJV are taken from The New King James Version. Copyright © 1979, 1980, 1982, Thomas Nelson, Inc; NASB are taken from the *New American Standard Bible.* Copyright © The Lockman Foundation 1960, 1995. Used by permission; THE MESSAGE are taken from *The Message,* copyright © by Eugene H. Peterson, 1993, 1994, 1995, 1996. Used by permission of NavPress Publishing Group; NLT are taken from the *Holy Bible, New Living Translation,* copyright © 1996 by Tyndale Charitable Trust. Used by permission of Tyndale House Publishers.

ISBN 978-1-56292-160-6

© 2004 BORDON BOOKS
© 2004 COOK COMMUNICATIONS MINISTRIES
Developed by Bordon Books

TManuscript written by Gena Maselli.
Cover Photo: © Stockbyte

Printed in the United States of America
First Edition 2004

3 4 5 6 7 8 9 10

051608

INTRODUCTION

Life is serious. And life as a teen is something God takes very seriously. Separating yourself from the world and its way of doing things is often difficult. But God wants you set apart for Him—unplugged from the deception of the world so that you can see God's better plan—*Truth Unplugged.*

What? You don't really believe it?

Put the biblical teen David in front of Goliath and have him hurl stones at the speed of a bullet to break a stalemate that no adult in his time could manage. Or how about this? Send the Son of God to Earth as a helpless baby, and make Him the sole, 24/7 responsibility of a fourteen- to sixteen-year-old mother named Mary. Or call a shy, sensitive teen named Jeremiah, and tell him to be the bearer of bad news to a king and his court—adults whose lives are way out of control. Oh, and tell him these people will hate him and never listen to him.

Yes, God really does take teens seriously—and that includes *you!*

Youth for God is just another name for serious, out-of-the-box adventurers. You are dealing with important, life-altering issues every day—stuff your parents may know nothing about. And the decisions you make are often under pressures that would make any adult cave. But you can't cave. You have your whole future ahead of you—and you plan to make it a good one. That's why it's so important to have God's reality—His *Truth Unplugged* for your life.

So here are some stories dealing with some pretty heavy stuff—stories about decisive moments in lives that look a lot like yours. At the end of each story, we've included a verse from the Bible, just so you know what God has to say about your issues—a **Download** of what He wants to say to you. Then there is a **Truth Link**—a prayer that can help you tell God what you need and really say it like it is.

In **Power Up** you will find questions or challenges that will hold you accountable for your decisions and help you see impli- cations that aren't always obvious. Sometimes you might feel like

Power Up is in your face, but it will bring the truth to you from a very honest perspective and hopefully give you a true reflection of your heart.

Finally, there is **Truth Unplugged**—a rule of thumb to help you remember what to do when life is moving a little fast and furious and someone is tapping his or her foot, pushing you to go a certain way. It can help you go God's way. Because, like we said, your life is serious business, so serious that sometimes you are the only one God can count on to do the right thing.

Don't let anyone put you down because you're young.
1 Timothy 4:12

TABLE OF CONTENTS

Introduction 5

The Challenge (Mentoring)...9

No-man's-land (Divorce)...15

Explosions (Anger)...20

Family Keys (Family Changes) 25

What's the Big Deal? (Drugs) 30

The Awakening (Drinking) 36

Stick with It (Diligence) 42

His Brother's Secret (Joy) 47

Plan B (Pride) 51

Blindsided (Rejection) 57

Not the End of the World (Peace)................................62

The Fall Guy (Forgiveness) 68

The Right Place for Now (Decision-making) 73

The Best Birthday Present Ever (Love) 78

The Double Life (Church) 82

The Accident (Trusting God) 88

The Intruder (Jealousy)..94

The Unexpected Hero (Inner Strength) 99

Black and White (Honor)..103

The Proof of Life (Prayer)...108

The Sacrifice (Giving) 113

No One Will Ever Know (Sex)......................................118

The Reality of It All (Fantasy).....................................124

Turn on the Light (Encouragement) 130

The Grace to Live at Home (Difficult Parents)...........135

Right before My Eyes (Pornography) 141

Making the Time Count (Attitude)...............................146

The New Pecking Order (Persecution)........................151

Dirt, Cobwebs, and More Dirt (Faithfulness) 156

Get Outta My Life! (Sibling Rivalry) 161

We're in This Together (**Illness**) 167

Getting the Whole Story (**Criticism**) 172

Got It Pretty Good (**Thankfulness**) 177

Watch That Mouth (**Profanity**) 183

Better than You Can Imagine (**Death**) 189

The Driving Dilemma (**Patience**) 194

Worthless (**Suicide**) 199

The Easy Way Out (**Lying**)...204

Man vs. Machine (**Materialism**) 210

What about *Them?* (**Racism**)..215

Nudges (**Holy Spirit**) 220

The Last Laugh (**Bullying**)..225

Backpedaling (**Bragging**)...231

Truth in the Fog (**Masturbation**) 237

But I Didn't Mean To . . . (**Responsibility**) 242

A World of Difference (**Salvation**) 247

Topical Index 255

THE CHALLENGE

Mentoring

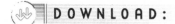

DOWNLOAD:

Pass on what you heard from me . . . to reliable leaders who are competent to teach others. 2 Timothy 2:2

Randy Martin stood at the edge of the field, watching the kids throw the baseball back and forth. Most of the time they missed it and had to retrieve it from under the bushes. They were possibly the worse baseball team Randy had ever witnessed.

He couldn't believe his dad had forced him to volunteer to coach this community Little League team. His dad's words still rang in his ears: "You need to take some responsibility and realize that the world doesn't revolve around you."

Whatever, Randy thought.

The truth—it was punishment for some of Randy's latest escapades. Last week, he had taken his father's truck without permission. He had only gone to a friend's house, but his dad wasn't amused. And then there was the little "miscommunication" with his parents the week before that. He'd told them he was going to a friend's house. Instead, he and his friends went to a party across town—and stayed out all night. By the time Randy returned home, his father was panicked and furious. He had spent the night driving all over the city looking for Randy. He had called the police and all of Randy's friends. It wasn't pretty.

So in return for those incidents, Mr. Martin decided that Randy had too much time on his hands and needed something constructive to do. After a few phone calls, Randy's father had volunteered him to help coach an inner-city Little League team. Randy had played baseball for years, first in independent Little League and now in high school. Over the years, he had played all the positions and had attended numerous baseball camps and practices.

According to his coaches, if Randy stayed on his present course, he could possibly get a college scholarship. Mr. Martin doubted that would happen if Randy didn't curb his other "extracurricular activities." So to ensure that his son stayed on the straight and narrow, Randy was to coach this pathetic little team four nights a week following his own practices.

"Hey, you the coach?" one boy asked cynically, eyeing Randy's letter jacket.

"Yup. That's me. Coach Randy," he responded with more than a little sarcasm.

"You don't look like much," the boy smirked. "Do you even *know* how to play baseball, or do you just say you do to get girls?"

"Trust me, I know how to play," Randy said defensively. *Who does this little squirt think he is anyway?* Randy thought. *I can catch, hit, slide, and pitch circles around these twerps.*

"We'll see," the boy muttered as he walked off toward the other players.

Randy gathered his new team for introductions. He counted twelve boys, ages nine and ten, including the one he had already met, Ty. All were dressed in old tattered clothes and had on even older equipment. Though they were young, Randy knew some of these kids were quite a bit older in life experience due to hardship. They were tough—tougher than Randy had been at their age, quite possibly tougher than he was at that moment.

After the introductions, Randy had the boys take the field for practice drills. Within minutes, Randy realized he needed to start with the basics—how to throw and catch. Some didn't even know the rules of the game. *Boy, I've got my work cut out for me,* he thought.

By the end of practice, everyone was exhausted, especially Randy. He wasn't used to being in charge of twelve boys, all demanding his attention. They continually asked questions and distracted each other; many just goofed off. What should have taken thirty minutes to explain and practice took over an hour. Watching them go home, Randy wondered if he could handle this.

"So are you gonna be here tomorrow, or are you gonna ditch us?" Ty asked skeptically.

"I'll be here," Randy said weakly as he turned to face Ty, wondering how this kid could read him so well. "What makes you think I won't?"

"You just don't look like you want to be here, like you're doing this because you have to."

Inwardly, Randy was shocked that this kid could see right through. Taking up the challenge, he asserted, "I'll be here."

Over the next few weeks, Randy worked with the team. Although they weren't major-league material, they did improve. By the end of their second game, their record was 1-1. Not bad for a team of beginners.

What surprised Randy more than anything was how much he enjoyed getting to know the boys. At first, they barely spoke to him about anything other than baseball, but as the weeks went on, they came to him with a variety of questions, everything from faith and family issues to school and girls. Repeatedly Randy heard himself say the things his father had been saying to him. He talked to them about responsibility and sportsmanship. He corrected them when they cursed or put each other down. He became more than just a baseball coach; he became a surrogate big brother.

Following one of the games, Ty approached him. "Hey Coach, you got a minute?"

Randy waited to hear what Ty had to say. Of all the boys, Ty had been the hardest to reach. Slowly, he had started to trust Randy, but the progress was very, very gradual. It was just Ty and his mother. He had never known his father, and he carried the burden of the "man of the house" very seriously.

"Coach, I got a question for you," he hesitated. "I gotta do a paper at school about the man I admire the most. And—well—I thought about it, and that's you."

Randy didn't know what to say. Touched and embarrassed, he said, "Ty, that's really cool. I'm honored. Thanks."

"Yeah, well, I gotta ask you some questions about the qualities I admire and how someone like me can develop them," Ty continued.

"Sure, I'll answer your questions. Why don't we get together after practice tomorrow? We'll go to Baskin Robbins for an ice cream cone, my treat," Randy offered.

"Okay," Ty said with a glimmer in his eye. "I like ice cream."

Following Monday's practice, Randy and Ty enjoyed double-scoop ice cream cones while Ty asked Randy questions. He asked why Randy had become a coach, which Randy answered honestly. He asked what he enjoyed about coaching and why he continued to do it.

After thinking about it for a few minutes, Randy responded, "I like the guys. They have a lot of potential, not just at baseball, but as kids. I like being a part of their lives and watching them grow."

Ty listened and slowly asked, "You think *I* got potential?"

Randy laughed, "Ty you have more potential than any kid I've ever met. I mean that."

Ty beamed as he finished his ice cream.

Later at home, Randy thought about his time with Ty and the rest of the boys. He couldn't believe that only a few weeks ago he had considered it a punishment to teach them. Now, it was a bright spot in his day. He loved the idea that what he said and did with these boys counted. Who'd have thought that he could be someone they would look up to and want to be like one day.

TRUTH UNPLUGGED:

Look for opportunities to be an example—a mentor—of Christ's love, goodness, and wisdom to others.

He thought back to his first day when Ty asked him if he would continue to be their coach. Randy had taken his question as a challenge, and he was so glad he had.

TRUTH LINK:

Dear Lord, I want to pass on the same love, goodness, and wisdom to others that You've shown to me. Help me to see opportunities where I can give to others by instructing and encouraging them. Help me to be a mentor for You. Amen.

POWER UP:

Can you think of people who have influenced how you act or think? A parent? A coach? An older brother or sister? A teacher? Maybe they didn't even say anything directly, but you learned just by watching them. You may think mentoring is reserved for older people, but it's not. If you consider how much you pass on to your younger brothers, sisters, or friends, you'll realize that mentoring is something you do every day. It's powerful. It means showing someone else the love of Jesus through your actions and your words. It's about helping them become the people God desires them to be.

NO-MAN'S-LAND

Divorce

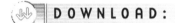

DOWNLOAD:

"I know the plans I have for you," declares the Lord, "plans to prosper you and not to harm you, plans to give you hope and a future." Jeremiah 29:11 NIV

"So, when is your dad coming to pick you up?" Mike's mother asked, standing in his bedroom doorway.

"He said he'd be here around 6:30," Mike responded, packing his bag for a weekend with his father.

"Is she going to be there?"

"Who?"

"Little Miss Aerobics Instructor," Mike's mother sneered.

"I don't know, Mom," Mike said with resignation. *When will this ever end?* he silently sighed.

"Well, she's so young she probably still has a curfew. Even if she is there, she probably won't be able to stay long."

Mike's parents had divorced the previous year. It hadn't come as a surprise since their home had been a war zone for years, full of screaming matches followed by frosty silence. Mike preferred the screaming. At least then he understood his place in the mix. The silent conflicts had crept into every corner of the house, making it impossible for him to relax even now, months after his father had moved out.

After his parents' divorce, Mike thought it would get better. At least if they weren't living together, there would be peace, he had reasoned. That proved to be an illusion.

Mike now lived in "no-man's-land" between the two rivals. He spent every other weekend and one or two dinners a week with his dad. The rest of the time he lived with his mom.

His parents didn't talk to each other anymore. Instead, they talked through Mike or their lawyers. Through Mike, they tried to find out as much as possible about the other. Whom the other dated. How much money the other had. What kind of things the other did for Mike. One another's jobs. Anything and everything. They congratulated themselves when they discovered that the other was having difficulty. Mike's mom was convinced that his dad was in the midst of a midlife crisis, and his dad was equally certain that his mother had become a nagging shrew who didn't know how to have a good time.

Mike didn't see either of them that way. They just approached life differently. His levelheaded mother preferred simplicity and frugality. His generous father, always the life of the party, thrived on spontaneity. Mike loved them both, but found it difficult being stuck in the middle.

He tried not to dwell on whether or not they had regrets about having him. *If I hadn't been born,* he reasoned, *they would be able to get on with their lives without having to see each other again. But because of me, they are stuck with a connection to each other forever.*

Mike shook his head, trying to escape that harassing thought. He continued stuffing clothes and toiletries into his bag. His mom was still complaining about his father and his father's young girlfriend.

"I just can't believe he's not embarrassed to date her. She's half his age," she said and then mumbled, "but what do I know? I lived with him for seventeen years, and I still don't understand him."

A horn honked, abruptly interrupting her. She walked to the window. "He's here."

"I'm ready."

"Do you have your jacket?" she asked. "It could get chilly this weekend. Oh, and by the way, I'll be over at Grandma's tomorrow, so if you need me, call me over there. I love you, Mike," she said giving him a hug. "Have fun."

"I love you too, Mom. I'll see you on Sunday." Mike grabbed his jacket and bag, then walked out the door.

"Hey, Sport," his dad called, opening the truck door from the inside. "Guess what we're going to do?" Too excited to wait for a reply, he continued. "We're going boating! I have a friend at work who invited us out to his place for the weekend. He lives on Lake Kipaushee. He has a motorboat, so we can tear around the lake. And we're gonna cook out. It'll be a blast. Come on, jump in. We can head out there now."

"Cool, dad, sounds like fun."

As they drove away, Mike's dad asked him about friends and school. Then the conversation turned to his mother.

TRUTH UNPLUGGED:

Although things in your life may be difficult now, God's picture of your future is full of great things.

"How's your mom?"

Here it comes, Mike thought. "She's fine."

"She got big plans this weekend?" he smirked. "Don't answer that. As if your mother *ever* has big plans. She'll probably just sit home alone and read a book."

Mike turned and stared out the window.

"Hey, I'm just playing around," his dad said, tapping Mike on the chest.

"No, you're not," Mike said quietly under his breath.

"What was that?"

Turning to face his father, he spoke evenly, "You're not joking, Dad. You and Mom never joke about each other. You just trash each other. You used to trash each other face-to-face. Now you just trash each other to me."

Mike's dad stared straight ahead.

"You guys probably wish I'd never been born, so you could be rid of each other," Mike murmured, turning back toward the window.

Mike's dad shot him a surprised look. "What'd you just say?"

"I said you probably wish I'd never been born, so you could be rid of each other once and for all."

Mike's dad pulled his truck over to the side of the road, allowing other cars to fly by. He turned to his son, "Mike, I want you to hear me on this. Your mother and I have *never* wished you hadn't been born. I know things have been tough between us, but there's one thing we agree on, and that's you. You are the best thing that has ever happened to either of us. And I'm sorry if our bickering has made you think you are anything but a gift to us."

Mike didn't say anything. He stared down at his hands, trying to keep tears from coming to his eyes.

"I'll tell you what," his dad continued in a strained voice, "I'll call your mom. I'm not promising that we'll be perfect, but I'll talk to her about how we can work together to keep you out of our problems."

Then, grabbing Mike in a bear hug, he choked, "I love you, Mike. Don't you ever doubt that you're the best thing in my life."

TRUTH LINK:

Dear Lord, please help me to live in peace in my home. Show me how to be an example to my family and how to approach each day the way You want me to. I know You love me. Help me not to entertain thoughts that life would be better without me, but to remember that You have good plans for my life. Amen.

POWER UP:

Have you lived in the aftermath of an ugly divorce? Or maybe your parents are divorced, but on somewhat friendly terms. Even better, maybe your parents are happily married. If so, great. Unfortunately, that's not how it is for many others. With some divorced parents, the battle continues to rage, leaving kids feeling caught in the middle. If that's you, ask God to show you how to live and respond to their anger in love and peace. Allow Him to show you how to be an example, and refuse to give in to thoughts that their problems are your fault or that life would be better off without you. God planned your life from the beginning, and He still has good plans for you. Your future is bright!

EXPLOSIONS

Anger

Be quick to listen, slow to speak and slow to become angry, for man's anger does not bring about the righteous life that God desires. James 1:19-20 NIV

"Augh! Stupid game!" Sam threw the Xbox controller onto the floor.

Startled, his seven-year-old brother, Drew, stopped playing with Bailey, the family dog. He curiously watched Sam's reaction.

"What's wrong?" his mother called from the kitchen.

"Nothing!" Sam responded angrily. "Sometimes I just can't stand this game. It doesn't move the way I want it to, and all my guys get killed."

"If it makes you that mad, you need to put it away," his mother counseled.

Sam ignored his mother's words and thought, *She just doesn't understand. It doesn't matter if I get angry at a stupid game. So what if I lose my temper sometimes? It happens to everyone.*

The next day in gym class, Sam and his friends were playing basketball. It was four against four, and though they played as hard as they could, Sam's team was still down by eight points. *This is ridiculous!* Sam screamed inside. *What's wrong with everyone?*

After a few more shots, his team was down by twelve points.

"You guys, get it together!" Sam yelled at his teammates.

"Hey man, calm down; it's just a game," his friend Justin said. "Nobody's keeping track."

"Lose on your own time," Sam shot back. "I play to win." With that, Sam ran to steal the ball from Kurt, his friend and opponent, and in the process slammed him to the ground.

In a flash, Kurt was back on his feet, coming after Sam. "What's your problem, man?" Kurt roared, shoving Sam from the back, causing him to fall to his knees. "This is supposed to be a friendly game!"

In a split second, Sam and Kurt faced off, shoving each other back and forth. Just as Sam started to throw the first punch, Coach Walker came up. "Sam! Kurt! You know the rules. No fighting. If you have that much energy, you can run for the rest of class. If I see it happen again, you'll take a trip to Principal Tyner's office—probably even get suspended. Think about that while you're running. Now, move!"

For the next fifteen minutes, Sam and Kurt ran laps around the gym.

Later in the locker room, Justin came up while Sam was finishing getting dressed. "Man, what's up with you? You went way overboard."

"What did I do? I didn't mean to knock him down," Sam said without remorse. "I just hate to lose. We could have had that game if everyone had stopped playing like idiots."

"Yeah, well, the guys don't want to play with you anymore. You fly off the handle at the smallest thing and take it out on everyone. All we want to do is play a simple game, and you treat it like the NBA playoffs."

"Whatever. I'm just serious about it."

"Fine. Just find another group to be serious with, 'cause we're not playing with a hothead."

Sam thought about what Justin said. *Why is everyone on my case lately? I was just being competitive. Was that so wrong? If they can't take it, they should stay off the court,* Sam fumed.

Leaving gym class, Sam headed to meet Mindy, his girlfriend, for lunch. He saw her standing next to the vending machines talking to Craig Wallace, her ex-boyfriend. All of a sudden, Sam saw red.

Who does Craig think he is, making a play for Mindy? She dumped the jerk over the summer. He needs to be reminded of that fact, he argued to himself.

Walking up, he slung an arm around Mindy's shoulders and glared at Craig. Confused, Craig looked from Mindy to Sam and back again.

"Uh, look, Mindy, I'll catch you later. If you think about it, I'd love to see that book we talked about."

"If you need a book, maybe you should hit the library," Sam challenged.

"Sam, Craig and I were just talking about . . ." Mindy tried to explain.

"Yeah, I got that much. But maybe Craig can hit on somebody else's girlfriend next time."

Surprised at Sam's reaction, Craig held up his hands in surrender, shaking his head as he walked away.

Mindy turned on Sam, her eyes blazing. "What was that about?"

"I just don't want that loser making a play for my girlfriend."

"Craig and I are friends. He wasn't hitting on me. He asked if he could borrow a book. And here's a news flash, Sam—you don't own me. Keep it up, and I'll be *your* ex-girlfriend too." With that, Mindy stormed off, leaving Sam in the hallway, alone.

What is everyone's problem? he wondered. *I defended myself, and all of a sudden people are acting like I'm the idiot.* Shaking his head, he went to get some lunch.

After school Sam went home. As he opened the front door, he heard Drew yelling at the dog. "Stupid dog!" Drew yelled, reaching to slap Bailey.

TRUTH UNPLUGGED:

You don't have to be like a volcano, ready to explode when difficult situations come up. God can help you deal with feelings of anger. Ask Him.

"Hey, Drew, what's up? You know better than to hit Bailey. What'd he do anyway?"

"I told him to sit, and he won't! He makes me so mad!"

Suddenly, Sam stopped. Hadn't he said those same words yesterday while playing Xbox? Lately he often felt like hitting something too.

Is this what I sound like? Sam wondered, taking a seat on the edge of the couch.

"Maybe you should walk away when you start to feel like hitting something," Sam offered, remembering what his mother had said to him.

"That's not what *you* do!" Drew insisted.

"No, lately I haven't. But I'm gonna try harder."

Drew seemed appeased with Sam's suggestion. Picking up Bailey, Drew went to play in the backyard. As they went, Sam thought about how out of control he'd been—losing his temper over even small things. He thought of all the apologies he owed to Justin, Kurt, Mindy, and, yes, even Craig.

God, help me with that one, he thought with a sigh.

TRUTH LINK:

Dear Lord, I have a problem with anger. Even little things set me off. I try to control my temper, but sometimes it still gets the best of me. Please help me to respond with self-control when dealing with other people and things. And when I do get angry, help me to walk away from the situation rather than act on it. Ame

POWER UP:

Do you have a temper? Do you become so angry sometimes that you just want to throw something or hurt someone? God can help you develop more patience, show you what triggers your anger, and teach you how to deal with it. He can show you how to stay calm and walk away from irritating situations. Remember, walking away isn't cowardice. In fact, it takes more strength and character to walk away than it does to allow anger to get the best of you.

FAMILY KEYS

Family Changes

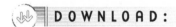 **DOWNLOAD:**

Let petitions and praises shape your worries into prayers, letting God know your concerns. Before you know it, a sense of God's wholeness, everything coming together for good, will come and settle you down. Philippians 4:6-7

Jack looked at the view from the top of the lighthouse. The gray ocean stretched forward and from each side meeting the heavy, gray sky in the distance. The sea rolled and tossed. White caps raced one after another toward the rocky shore.

This was the coolest thing he'd seen on the trip. Jack hadn't wanted to come on this trip with his father, new stepmother, and new stepsister. He'd rather have stayed at home with his friends, enjoying a hot summer of swimming in the lake. Instead he was forced to join these strange people his father had invited into their lives.

"The Cape Hatteras Lighthouse is the tallest lighthouse in the United States, standing 208 feet tall," the rugged-faced guide explained. "Its purpose is to help ships navigate the treacherous waters of the Diamond Shoals off our North Carolina coast."

Jack looked over at his father, who watched the guide with intensity. That's the way his dad faced every situation—with intensity. Even this vacation was intense. His dad had married Marie three months ago. And with Marie came Samantha, Jack's new ten-year-old stepsister. Jack's dad decided they all needed a vacation to bond as a family.

Jack choked at the thought. The last thing he wanted was to "bond" with these strangers. He turned to stare out at the water again. *Why did he have to get married?* he wondered again. *We were just fine without them.*

"Hey, Jack, you ready to go? Marie and Samantha want to go to the gift shop," his dad said, coming up beside him.

"Yeah, Dad, whatever," Jack said hopelessly.

"Hey, what's this about? Aren't you having a good time?" his dad asked enthusiastically.

"Sure, Dad, the lighthouse is really cool."

"Good. Once we leave here, we'll go into town to a historical bed and breakfast that Marie and Samantha found. Then we will find a restaurant that serves some awesome seafood. It'll be great."

Jack didn't comment. Instead, he started down the stairs, wishing they could stay in the kind of place he and his dad usually stayed in—a chain hotel. For dinner, they would have ordered out for pizza while watching an action adventure movie on Pay Per View. Instead, he faced a night of weird food and frilly rooms with no TV.

Ugh! Could this trip get any worse? he wondered.

Down in the gift shop, Marie and Samantha announced the find of the perfect souvenir for the trip—matching T-shirts. They each held up a T-shirt with a big picture of the black and white candy-striped lighthouse on the front. They were on sale, four for thirty-five dollars.

"We can all match!" Samantha squealed.

"Um—I think I'll pass," Jack mumbled, trying hard not to sound completely horrified at the thought of wearing the T-shirt, let alone matching the others.

"What do you mean?" Samantha asked in shock.

"Sorry, Sammie. I'm *not* wearing *that* T-shirt," Jack said sarcastically.

"My name's *Samantha!* And I wouldn't want to match you anyway," she cried. "I thought having a brother would be cool, but you're just a jerk!" Throwing down the T-shirt, she ran out of the store.

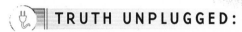

TRUTH UNPLUGGED:

God wants to show you His perspective. He can give you hope through changes in your family.

Marie looked at Jack and then at his dad. Without saying a word, she placed the T-shirts back on the display and headed out to comfort Samantha.

Stunned, Jack didn't know what to do. He'd never experienced a sister's fury before. "What's with her? All I said was that I didn't want one of these stupid T-shirts. She didn't have to go tragic on me," Jack said defensively.

His dad exhaled slowly. "Jack, this marriage is an adjustment for everyone, not just you. You're getting used to a new stepmom and stepsister. I have a new wife and daughter. Marie's getting used to us, and so is Samantha. You know, Marie told me that Samantha has always wanted a big brother. So to her, you're an answer to prayer. But instead of trying to get to know her, you brush her aside every chance you get."

Jack felt defeated. He hadn't thought of it from anyone else's perspective. He just knew things were difficult for him. "I just miss the way things used to be," he mumbled.

"Actually, Jack, I think things were better in your mind than they were in reality. Do you realize that since Marie and I have been married, we've eaten almost every dinner at the dining room table, like a real family? I know more about what's happening with you now than I ever did before. And Marie goes out of her way to make sure you have the right clothes for school and sports. She reminds me about all of your games and school activities so I can be there. And on top of that, she and Samantha haven't missed one of your games yet. You've gone from zero or only one person in the stands to three people at every game, cheering their hearts out. Trust me; you have much more now than you did before. You just won't let yourself admit it."

Jack considered what his dad said. Maybe he was right. Maybe he had made things better in his mind than they really had been before Marie and Samantha came into their lives. Actually, he hadn't even noticed all the nice things they had done for him or how much nicer things were with them there. He had been too busy avoiding them.

After his dad left the shop, Jack decided to make more of an effort with his new family. Maybe things weren't so bad after all. Then he thought of a way to make things up to Samantha. Glancing around the store, he found exactly what he was searching for.

Back at the car, Jack crawled into the backseat. Refusing to look at him, Samantha stared out the window, her face streaked with dried tears.

"Hey, Samantha, I found something for you," he said. His father and Marie turned around to listen.

"Actually," he continued, "I found something for everyone."

She cautiously turned toward him. "What?"

"Well, it's not a T-shirt, but I think it's pretty cool." Then out of a bag, Jack pulled four bronze-colored key chains in the shape of the lighthouse. "They're key chains from Cape Hatteras Lighthouse. We can put our house keys on them. See, we could only wear a T-shirt once in a while, but we can use these key chains every day. And we'll be the only ones with these key chains and keys to our house on them."

Samantha reached out and gently took her key chain, examining it in her hands. "It's just for us?" she asked.

"Yeah, just for our family," Jack said, smiling at her.

"Jack?" she asked. "You can call me Sammie, if you want."

He smiled, "I think that would be a pretty cool—my own big-brother name for you."

Samantha smiled and giggled as she grasped her new light-house key chain.

TRUTH LINK:

Dear Lord, my family has recently changed. I don't understand why it had to change, but I ask You to give me peace and wisdom during the transition. Help me to be patient with my new family members, and help me see the good things about them. Help me to love them the way You love them. Amen.

POWER UP:

Families are complex, and it's especially difficult when step-parents, stepbrothers, and stepsisters enter your family picture. It's easy to resent the changes that they bring to your life. Things used to be one way, and now they're another. Remember that it's a change for everyone—your parent, your new step-parent, your siblings, and your new stepsiblings. It's important for everyone to find the best way to live together.

Talk to your parents about your concerns, and then really listen to what they have to say. Try to be patient, and pray for God to help you during the transition. He can help you make your way through it and give you better understanding concerning it.

WHAT'S THE BIG DEAL?

Drugs

DOWNLOAD:

I call heaven and earth to witness against you today, that I have set before you life and death, the blessing and the curse. So choose life in order that you may live, you and your descendants, by loving the Lord your God, by obeying His voice, and by holding fast to Him; for this is your life and the length of your days. Deuteronomy 30:19-20 NASB

"Come on. It's just pot," Trevor pleaded, holding a small plastic bag containing two joints.

Sitting in his bedroom on a Saturday afternoon, Rob listened, remembering all the things he'd heard about drugs. He could hear his dad asking him to promise he'd never get into them. He could see his mother shaking her head when his cousin entered yet another drug rehab center. *But does any of that really apply to this?* he wondered. *It is just pot*, he reasoned.

"Where'd you get it?" Rob asked.

"My brother gave it to me. He said it's harmless—just makes you feel really relaxed. It's no big deal—not like cocaine or heroine or anything like that," Trevor explained.

Although Rob had never considered doing drugs before, he had to admit he was curious about what it was like. And Trevor had a point; it was just marijuana. It wasn't the bad stuff. Maybe he'd give it a try. "Okay, I'll try it," he finally said.

"Cool. I didn't want to do it without my best bud," Trevor said excitedly. "That's why my brother gave me two; although, we can just smoke the first one together."

During the next twenty minutes, Rob and Trevor shared a joint, enjoying the euphoric sensation that washed over them. Then they felt a ravenous hunger take hold and raided the kitchen for munchies.

After Trevor had gone home, Rob thought about the day. Smoking marijuana wasn't what he had expected. He'd been scared that something terrible would happen, like getting sick or freaking out. But it didn't. He decided that maybe Trevor and his brother were right; *Maybe pot isn't such a big deal after all.*

Remembering that his parents were due home within the hour, Rob opened his bedroom windows, sprayed air freshener throughout the house, and rushed to clean up the kitchen. He finished just five minutes before he heard the garage door open, signaling his parents' return home after a day of running errands. His mother walked into the house and set grocery bags on the kitchen counter.

"Hey, Rob, can you help your dad bring in the rest of the bags?" his mother asked offhandedly as she began to put groceries away. "We decided to have fajitas tonight. You can invite Trevor over if you want," she offered, heading to the thermostat. "Why is it so hot in here?" Then wrinkling her nose, she asked, "And what's that smell?"

Rob hesitated a second before answering. His mind raced. He'd tried so hard to make things appear and smell normal around the house. "Uh—I opened the windows for a little while this afternoon. It felt kinda stuffy in here, like it needed to be aired out. That's probably all it is."

His mother adjusted the temperature and looked around. "Did you clean?"

"Yeah, I picked up a little," Rob said as he headed out the door to help his father.

With the rest of the bags, he and his father made their way into the house. As soon as his father reached the kitchen door, he stopped. His muscles tensed. He set the bags on the floor; he walked through the living room and then down the hall. He stopped in front of Rob's bedroom, opened the door, and walked in.

Rob and his mother watched his dad. Rob tried to look unconcerned, but inwardly he was shaking. Then Rob's mother also entered the room. A few more seconds passed, and Rob heard mumbling from his room. *This is bad,* he thought desperately. *Why did I let Trevor talk me into this?*

"Rob, come in here," his dad called.

Slowly, Rob walked into his room. His mother sat on his bed with a stricken look on her face, as though she would faint at any moment. His dad stood with his back to the door, hands on his hips, looking out the window.

"Do you have something you want to say?" his father asked slowly, never turning to face him.

"No—well, I—uh . . . ," Rob stammered. His mind reeled trying to come up with the right thing to say.

As he tried to put words together, his father spoke in a deep low tone. He meant business. "Before you say something to make this situation worse," he said, "let me encourage you to tell the truth. So I'll ask you again, do you have something to tell me."

Shame washed over Rob. He dropped his gaze to the floor. In a rush, he began, "Trevor and I smoked marijuana today. He said it would be okay. Not a big deal. He said it wasn't a real drug."

His mother gasped, "Oh, Rob, no!" As if trying to wake from a bad dream, she shook her head and lowered her face into her hands.

His father stood rigid, "I've seen kids in my clinic who thought the same thing about marijuana." He looked at him in a way Rob had never experienced. He saw pain, disappointment, and fear in his dad's face. He knew he'd made a terrible mistake.

"Is this the first time you've experimented with drugs? And yes, marijuana is a real drug, regardless of what Trevor says. It can cause problems with memory, learning, lack of perception, and difficulty in thinking and problem solving. Research links it to respiratory problems, lung infections, and even cancer."

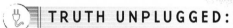 **TRUTH UNPLUGGED:**

Drugs take you down the wrong path—away from God and everything else that's important in your life. Choose life.

"Yes, I promise. It was the only time. I was just curious," Rob admitted dejectedly and then added, "Dad, I'll never do it again. I promise."

"I wish I could believe you, Rob, but we can't just ignore this. I love you, but at this point, I don't trust you," his father said.

Rob felt the weight of his choice. Over the next couple of hours, Rob and his parents sat around the dining room table and talked about the dangers of drugs. Then they discussed his punishment. They discussed his friendship with Trevor.

His father planned to call Trevor's parents the next day. Rob wouldn't be allowed to spend time alone with Trevor anymore. In fact, it would be a while before he would be allowed to stay home alone at all. And his parents decided he needed to visit his cousin at the drug treatment center so Rob could hear firsthand how drug addiction can destroy a life and a whole family.

By the end of the conversation, Rob was exhausted—physically, mentally, and emotionally. He had crossed over into a new place that day—a place he'd have given anything to never have gone. Now his parents didn't trust him. He had lost the precious gift of trust that they had once freely given and he had taken for granted.

As he lay down to sleep that night, he wondered how long it would take for his mom and dad to trust him again. He wondered what Trevor would say once his parents knew about the drugs. He'd probably be mad, and that only added to Rob's sadness.

His friendship with Trevor had changed too. His parents now viewed Trevor with suspicion. Although they hadn't said he and Trevor couldn't be friends, he knew they would prefer that Rob make other friends.

Rob knew that he'd lost a lot that day. Some of it he could earn back, but some, he realized, was lost forever. *It really did turn out to be a big deal after all,* he thought as he desperately tried to fall asleep.

TRUTH LINK:

Dear Lord, help me to stand strong against drugs so I won't give in to the temptation to take them. I want to stay on the right track in my life, and I realize that drugs are not any part of Your plan. Please, help me to be mindful of the consequences that my actions will produce and give me the strength to make the right decisions. Amen.

POWER UP:

Perhaps you've heard that for every action there is an equal and opposite reaction. It's true. You make choices every day that result in good or bad consequences. Drugs bring bad consequences—plain and simple. Aside from what they do to your health, they can consume every aspect of your life. Don't let anyone convince you they're harmless. They are not.

Or maybe you've been taking drugs and are making the decision to stop using them. If so, know that God will always forgive you and help you. You're never too far gone for Him to love you. Though your circumstances may not change immediately, He **WILL** help you face them.

THE AWAKENING

Drinking

DOWNLOAD:

"Be on your guard. Don't let the sharp edge of your expectation get dulled by parties and drinking and shopping."

Luke 21:34

The bright light shining down on Keith was painful. His eyes fluttered, and then he closed them again. Aching all over and feeling heavy, he just wanted to float down into the fog that threatened to engulf him.

"Keith, can you hear me? Come on, honey, open your eyes."

Keith heard his mother's frantic voice pleading with him. He couldn't tell exactly where she was, maybe somewhere near the light, but hearing her voice kept him from moving toward the fog. Instead, he tried to open his eyes again.

"Oh, Keith, we're here," his mother said as he opened his eyes. His mother and father stood on either side of him. Looking around, he saw that he was lying on a bed, dressed in some sort of gown, and had a tube coming out of his arm. He hurt every-where, especially across his chest.

Sliding his hand up to his chest, he tried to remove the weight that pressed down on him. His father gently took his hand. "Keith, you were in an accident. You're going to be okay. The seat belt saved you, but it left a nasty bruise. The doctors said you'll feel it for a while."

"Keith, do you remember what happened?" his mother asked.

"No," Keith said slowly. He tried to think of the last thing that happened. "I was over at Aaron's. He had a party."

"You and Aaron were in a car accident. Do you remember leaving Aaron's house?" his mother asked with worried eyes.

"No, the last thing I remember is being at Aaron's house. There were about ten of us hanging out at his pool," Keith explained.

His parents exchanged a look, and then his father patted his arm, "That's okay. We'll talk about it later. Why don't you get some rest now?"

Keith nodded and closed his eyes. Before he knew it, he was sound asleep.

The next morning Keith woke up feeling somewhat better. He was still sore, but at least he could focus his eyes without feeling too much pain. He looked around and realized he was in a hospital room. Although there was a bed next to his, he was the only patient in the room.

His chest still hurt, but there was no longer a tube connected to his arm. Lifting his gown, he saw the purplish stripe cut diag-onally across his chest. One of his forearms and a shoulder had a few bandages. Smaller bruises and scrapes covered his body, like he'd been tossed against a concrete wall at ninety miles per hour.

As he continued to examine his body, the door to his room opened, and his parents entered. They both looked exhausted, like they hadn't slept all night. His mother had been crying, and his father looked like he was on the verge of tears. They walked over to his bed.

His father cleared his throat before asking, "Hey champ, how are you feeling this morning?"

"Like I've been beat with a baseball bat," Keith said. "Are you guys okay? I'm sorry I worried you, but you said the doctors said I'd be okay."

His parents looked at each other again. His mother's eyes shimmered with tears.

His dad looked at him solemnly and asked, "Keith, last night you said you didn't remember what happened. Do you remember anything this morning?"

"Well, we were over at Aaron's. He had a party and there were about ten of us there. Then . . . " Keith tried to remember what happened next. "Aaron said he'd take me home. We got in his car. That's really all I remember."

"Keith, we know you and Aaron were drinking," his father said slowly, his eyes never leaving Keith's.

Slowly, Keith nodded his head. Though his parents had always warned him against drinking, he knew it wouldn't do any good to lie. "Yeah, one of the guys brought some beer to the party. Nothing big. We weren't drunk or anything."

His father closed his eyes and took a deep breathe. His mother stifled a cry.

Baffled, Keith looked from his father to his mother and back again. "It wasn't a big deal. I promise. I only had one beer. Aaron maybe had two."

Looking back at him, his father spoke in a strained voice, "Keith, the accident was bad. Aaron is in ICU. The doctors don't know if he's going to make it."

Keith felt the room begin to spin.

Aaron was his best friend. They had been inseparable since elementary school. They had been in the same classes and had gone to church camp together. Keith's father had taught them both how to parallel park. Aaron's dad had showed them how to tie a necktie. Their lives were connected.

"Can I see him?" he asked.

"I don't know, but I'll ask." His father slowly backed away from the bed and walked out of the room.

His mother reached for a chair, took a seat, and bowed her head. Keith knew she was praying silently, but he couldn't think straight enough to join her.

Why did this happen? he wondered desperately. *Only a couple of beers.* He kept repeating those words over and over in his mind. He and Aaron both knew better than to drink. And he'd heard the warning about drinking and driving, but they hadn't gotten drunk. In fact, Keith *never* got drunk, not like some of the other guys from school did. He only drank a beer or two when offered one at a party.

 TRUTH UNPLUGGED:

Don't let people—even your friends—talk you into drinking alcohol. Take a stand against it.

A few minutes later, his dad returned. "They said you can visit Aaron for a few minutes later this afternoon if you're feeling strong enough."

Late that day, Keith's father helped him into a wheelchair and wheeled him up to the ICU. Gazing through the observation window, Keith saw Aaron. His parents sat beside him as machines of all sizes beeped and blinked around him. Aaron lay pale and still with tubes running from him to the machines. Keith's dad opened the door and wheeled Keith to Aaron's bedside. Aaron's parents stepped back to make room for the wheelchair.

"I'll be right outside, his father said and quietly shut the door.

Keith sat there quietly, trying to grasp what was happening. It seemed so unreal. They had drunk only a little bit of alcohol. Large or small amounts—now it didn't matter. It had been enough to threaten their lives.

Keith laid his hand on Aaron's arm. "Don't give up, Aaron. You're too young to die, man. You fight, you hear?"

Then bowing his head, he prayed as Aaron's parents looked on, "God, please help Aaron. Please don't let him die. I'm sorry we were drinking. We won't ever drink again, but please save Aaron's life. I'll do anything—Please." By the end of the prayer, tears streamed down his face.

Two days later, Keith returned to the ICU to see Aaron again. Though still in critical condition, Aaron had improved. He had opened his eyes a few times and had squeezed his mother's hand.

Though Aaron was unconscious, Keith sat by his bed, telling him all about the latest news and sports scores. Then before he left, he prayed again, asking God to continue to heal Aaron, again promising that they would never drink again.

Just as he rose to leave, he heard Aaron move. Looking down at his friend, he saw that Aaron's eyes were open and watching him. Overwhelmed with relief, Keith smiled.

"Hey there, I've been waiting for you," he gulped back the tears. "You really scared me. I've never prayed so hard in my life! I've even promised God we'd never drink again if He'd heal you. And I'm here to tell you, it's one promise we're gonna keep. 'Cause if you ever scare me like this again, I'll kill you."

Aaron smiled and gently nodded his head.

Over the next few weeks, Aaron continued to improve. By week four, he was well enough to go home, though physical therapy was required for a while afterward. Keith made daily visits to see Aaron, hanging out with him or helping Aaron with his exercises. Though they'd been close friends for years, the two became even closer.

They'd faced death and then recovery together, and from then on, they took a stand against alcohol together.

And they kept their word about not drinking. After all they'd been through, it wasn't hard. The very thought of drinking was enough to make them sick.

TRUTH LINK:

Dear Lord, I don't want to drink, but there are a lot of people that I know—even close friends—who do. Please give me the strength to say no when someone offers me alcohol. Amen.

POWER UP:

You may have close friends who think it's fun to drink and get drunk. But drinking can impair your judgment or even kill you. Don't become deceived into thinking, **THAT'LL NEVER HAPPEN TO ME.** A large amount of alcohol in the blood has proven lethal to some teens. And many are killed each year from drunk driving or by the actions of those under the influence of alcohol.

Don't allow your friends to pressure you into making a detrimental, life-altering mistake. If you feel trapped, call a friend or your parents. Some taxi services even offer free rides to those who have been drinking. It's difficult to stand up to others and say no, but don't follow the crowd. Take a stand; it just may save your life.

STICK WITH IT

D i l i g e n c e

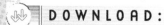

DOWNLOAD:

Easy come, easy go, but steady diligence pays off.

Proverbs 13:11

"Mark, I want to talk to you about your summer plans," his dad said as they sat down to dinner.

"Dad, it's only March. I don't know what I'm going to do yet."

"Well, that's why I want to talk to you about it now. You're almost sixteen, and you've been saying that you want a truck. If you do, you need to think about getting a job to earn money for it."

Mark stopped eating and stared at his dad. "I thought I was getting your old truck."

"Well, your mom and I have talked about it, and we've decided that you need to work for your vehicle. We know you're able to drive at sixteen, but we would feel better about you buying a vehicle with money that you earned rather than us just giving one to you. We think you'll appreciate it more," his dad explained.

Mark was shocked and irritated that his parents had decided he couldn't have his dad's old F150. He'd already planned to have it repainted and loaded with a new sound system. Disappointed, he pushed the rest of his dinner around on his plate. "Man, I'll never get a truck," he mumbled.

"Well, that's why I wanted to talk to you about it now. One of the guys I work with has a son who is a counselor at a nearby summer camp. There are two summer sessions—one in June and the other in July. You'd stay at the camp with the kids. The pay isn't great, but considering you wouldn't have to find transportation to and from work or be tempted to spend your earnings hanging out with your friends, you could have a pretty good amount saved by the end of the summer."

"It doesn't sound like much fun," Mark said.

"I don't think hanging out with little kids for a summer sounds so bad," his dad encouraged. "You'll get to take them swimming, canoeing, and other things you like to do anyway. Of course, you don't have to do it. But if you don't, you'll have to find something else. Whatever you decide, you need to make enough money to pay for the truck and your gas. Your mother and I will cover your insurance."

Mark hadn't even thought about what he'd do over summer vacation. He sure hadn't considered working all summer—especially with little kids. He knew this was what his father called "a defining moment" in his life—working for his first truck. Mark knew he didn't have to have a truck, but riding with his parents to school each day wasn't high on his list, and riding the school bus was definitely out of the question. He had to find a job.

For the next few days, Mark tried to think of alternatives to being a kids-camp counselor, but he couldn't come up with anything that was steady enough and didn't require him to get a ride to work every day. His parents' schedules were busy enough. They couldn't transport him to and from work at random hours.

Although he was disappointed that he wouldn't be able to see his friends all summer, he decided to send in his application for the camp counselor position.

At the end of April, after a phone interview and an in-person interview with the camp director, Mark was hired. Over the next month, he gathered all the stuff he needed—bug repellant, sunscreen, shorts, T-shirts, bathing suit, backpack, allergy medicine, etc. On June 1, his parents dropped him off at the camp. His mother hugged him fiercely and made him promise to call or write at least once a week. His dad slapped him on the back, saying, "You're going to have a great time, Mark. I'm really proud of you for doing this. And if you stick with it, you'll have the reward—your first truck. Trust me, it'll be worth it."

Mark tried to smile, but he felt disheartened. *Maybe I don't really need a truck after all,* he reasoned. Joining the other counselors for orientation, he learned the location of his cabin and his duties. He discovered that he would share a cabin with one other counselor. Together, they would be responsible for twenty boys each session.

As the camp director talked about the rules and schedule, Mark looked around. There were close to fifty counselors in the room—boys and girls who appeared to be his age. He recognized a few faces from school, but didn't really know anyone. *What have I gotten myself into?* he wondered. *Lord, give me strength.*

After the meeting ended, a tall guy who looked like he was a few years older than Mark came over. "Hey, man, my name's Seth. We're bunking together. This your first time?"

"Yeah, it is."

"Well, don't worry, this is my third year. Trust me, we're gonna have a blast," he beamed. "Every summer I can't wait to get back to these kids."

Though initially skeptical, Mark quickly discovered how fun and challenging his role as a camp counselor could be. Thankfully, he had Seth to show him the ropes. Seth, who was actually studying to be an outdoor adventure guide for children, took his role very seriously. He constantly encouraged Mark to "stick with it." If a kid had a hard day from homesickness, Seth would tell him to "stick with it" until the kid was laughing. If kids refused to do what they were supposed to do, Seth encouraged Mark to "stick with it" until they came around and did what they were supposed to do.

At the end of the two months, Mark was surprised to discover he was sad about leaving. It had been one of the best summers of his life. It hadn't been easy, but he'd finally learned how important it is to just "stick with it." In the end, he gained a lot. He now had a good start on his truck savings, and he learned that he really enjoyed working with kids.

TRUTH UNPLUGGED:

Make the decision to be diligent—to never give up—in your family, school, relationships, and job. The rewards will be well worth the effort.

Two months later, Mark turned sixteen, earned his driver's license, and bought his first truck. He had to admit that paying for it with his own money felt good. He didn't have enough money to upgrade the speakers or have it repainted, but Mark didn't mind. He was proud of the truck because it was his.

It was also the perfect vehicle to help with his new after-school job at the local community center. He was in charge of transporting canoes when they took boys to the lake. Balancing school, church, friends, and work wasn't easy, but he discovered that if he just "stuck with it" he could make it work. And the reward made the effort well worth it.

TRUTH LINK:

Dear Lord, I have something I need to do, but right now, it seems too hard to achieve it. I know I need to press forward and keep working toward my goal, but it would be easier to give up. Help me to be diligent. I want to become someone who is diligent in big things and small things, but I recognize that I need Your help. Amen.

POWER UP:

Have you ever thought about giving up or quitting something important? A job? School? A friendship? Or do you have a goal that seems so far away that you can't imagine attaining it, like buying a car or going to college? You will always have opportunities to give up when things seem hard or when goals appear too difficult to achieve, but don't do it. Make the decision to stick with it—be diligent. When you finally accomplish your goal, you'll discover just how rewarding it is, because you held on and accomplished the goal.

HIS BROTHER'S SECRET

Joy

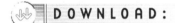 **DOWNLOAD:**

This day is holy to God. Don't feel bad. The joy of God is your strength! Nehemiah 8:10

Andrew walked in the front door to his house and heard laughter. In the living room, he found his twin brother, Alex, laughing hysterically at a Steve Martin movie. Dropping his backpack onto the living room floor, he stormed into the kitchen to get an after-school snack.

He couldn't understand how his brother could be so calm and nonchalant. Four weeks ago, their parents had told them they were getting a divorce. They had seen their dad only rarely since he moved out, and their mom was seldom home. She was usually at work, the lawyer's office, or church. Andrew and Alex weren't sure where they were going to live since their mom had said they would probably have to sell their house. They didn't even know if they could find another house in their school district.

To Andrew, everything seemed to be falling a part. He was angry and hurt. He'd thrown himself into school activities to avoid coming home. He'd always enjoyed working on the yearbook, but now he spent twice as much time as anyone else on it. People even joked that he was the yearbook's "one man show."

His brother, on the other hand, acted as if nothing was wrong. In fact, he acted goofier than ever. He'd always loved comedy. His dream was to become the next great stand-up comedian. He watched funny movies and stand-up comedians and even took drama in school, so he could learn "comedic timing," as he put it. The two brothers were on opposite ends of the spectrum. Andrew couldn't hide his anger and hurt, and Alex didn't seem to care.

"Hey, Andrew, do we have any Doritos left? I'm hungry," Alex said, walking into the kitchen and opening the pantry.

"Man, how do you do that?" Andrew spit out.

"Do what? Eat Doritos?" Alex asked with a smirk as he continued to search the pantry.

"No, act like nothing's wrong. Mom and Dad are getting a divorce. We might have to move and change schools, and you act like everything's normal. In fact, you act happy. I don't get it. Don't you even *care?*" Andrew's voice rose to a shout. He was angry and tired of being the only one who seemed to have a clue about what was really going on.

Alex stopped and closed the pantry. He turned to look at his brother, his face filled with hurt. It was the first time Andrew had seen him show anything close to emotion over their situation.

"Look, Andrew, I *know* what's happening. Trust me, I know what's happening. But I deal with it differently than you do. I'm trying to find some joy in my life right now instead of wallowing in anger and self-pity," he said.

"I'm not wallowing. And what joy? I don't see any joy around here," Andrew said, glaring at him.

Shrugging, Alex walked out of the kitchen, back to the living room, and turned the movie back on.

Andrew fumed, *He thinks he's so in control, trying to act like nothing's wrong.* Storming through the living room, he grabbed his backpack and retreated to his room. Unsure of what else to do, he sat on his bed, grabbed his pillow, and punched it. *Why can't they work things out? Why do they have to just give up and tear our family apart? And why does Alex handle it so well while I feel lost and alone?*

Caught up in his own thoughts, he almost didn't hear the knock on his door. "Andrew?" Alex called. "Can I come in?"

He didn't answer.

"Come on, Drew. Let me in," he called again.

Without saying a word, Andrew walked to the door and opened it. Then turning, he returned to his bed. Wearily, he watched Alex enter and sit down.

TRUTH UNPLUGGED:

You can walk in the joy of the Lord every moment of every day.

Looking at him, Alex said, "I'm sorry. I didn't mean to accuse you of wallowing. I just—I can tell you're having a hard time, and I know I can't really help you. I'm trying to keep my own head above water, ya know? That's why I pray every day for God's strength and joy. That's why I watch funny movies and try to laugh as much as possible."

"You seem like everything's no big deal," Andrew said quietly. "I feel like I'm the only one who cares about what's happening."

"No, you're not the only one. I care. But I know I can't change what's happening. I can't make Mom and Dad stay together. What I can do, though, is pray and try to stay happy—regardless of what else happens."

"What do you pray?" Andrew asked in earnest. "I've tried to pray, but I don't know what to ask for other than for God to make Mom and Dad change their minds."

"I pray for that, and I pray for the joy of the Lord to be my strength. It may sound simple, but that's all I know to do," he confided. "And ya know what? It's working. I really feel stronger and happier."

For the next few minutes, Andrew and Alex continued to talk about the whole situation. For the first time since their parents had announced their divorce, Andrew had someone to talk to, and he had some idea of what he could do. After they talked, they prayed. Together, they prayed for their parents to work out their problems. They prayed for each other to have joy, peace, and strength, regardless of what happened.

After they finished, they returned to the living room, ordered a pizza, and put on a funny Jackie Chan movie. Though Andrew always loved Jackie Chan flicks, he especially enjoyed this one— this time because he didn't have the weight of the world on his shoulders. He had finally discovered Alex's secret, and he was glad his brother had been willing to share it.

TRUTH LINK:

Dear Lord, I want Your joy to be my strength every day—not just when things are going well, but even when they aren't. I want my life to exhibit Your joy wherever I go and whatever I face. Please show me how to activate true joy in my life. Amen.

POWER UP:

Have you ever thought that some people are just born happy and others aren't? Well, although it comes more easily to some, that doesn't mean you can't be joyful every day. You can. By praying and reading your Bible, you can have the joy of the Lord too. As you turn to Him, He'll help you see life from His perspective when things go wrong, and He'll rejoice with you when things go right. And best of all, you'll realize that you don't have to handle everything on your own, because He's right there with you.

PLAN B

Pride

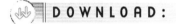

DOWNLOAD:

First pride, then the crash—the bigger the ego, the harder the fall. Proverbs 16:18

This is going to be a great year! Ryan thought as he drove to school with his sister, Lacy. It was the first day of his senior year. His summer had been a fun one, working for his dad's construction business. He had made enough money to purchase a great car. He had a beautiful girlfriend, and he was all set to step into the position of starting quarterback. It would be a great finale to his high school years.

"You look smug," Lacy said, eyeing him suspiciously, "What's up?"

"Nothing," he said. "I was just thinking about how great this year is going to be."

"Oh brother, the big-man-on-campus complex has started already," Lacy said, raising her eyebrows. "Just remember, I knew you when you were ten and puking your guts out from food poisoning. So don't get too high and mighty."

Ryan cut his eyes at her before pulling into the school parking lot. Just then, he saw Theresa, his girlfriend, waiting for him. They had known each other for years, but last year, their friendship had stepped up to dating each other. Most of last year, she had dated Corey Henderson, but when they broke up, Ryan was waiting. He asked her out at the beginning of the summer, and they had been together ever since.

Everyone said they looked great together. Theresa could have been a swimsuit model, and many people told Ryan that he looked like a young Tom Cruise. To Ryan, they were the perfect couple. He liked having a gorgeous girlfriend who made him look good. It fit his image, and to him image was everything.

"Hey, Ryan. I waited for you," Theresa said excitedly as Ryan arrived. "I thought it would really be good for us to make our entrance together. I mean, I know everyone knows we're together, but if we walk in together, it'll really make an impression. Oh, and I'm glad you wore that shirt. It really shows off your tan, and it goes with my outfit too. It wouldn't be good if we clashed, but then again, we couldn't exactly match either."

Lacy walked between them and turned to Ryan. "Oh brother," she said under her breath.

Throughout the day, Ryan was more and more convinced that this year would be the best. People complimented his tan and his car, and his classes would be a breeze since he'd finished most of his tough ones last year. All he had left was football.

After changing clothes, he made his way to the field. Ryan noticed a few new faces. The coach talked to one in particular, a new player named Chett Wilson, who had transferred from the school across town. He had played quarterback at his last school. Ryan and Chett were to compete for the same position, but Ryan wasn't nervous. As far as he was concerned, he was a shoo-in for quarterback.

"Ryan, can you come over here?" Coach Yancy asked. "You know Chett Wilson."

Ryan and Chett exchanged greetings.

Coach Yancy continued, "Since you're both used to playing quarterback, I want to take a look at both of you. I'm really glad that we're going to have two strong quarterbacks, but as you know, only one of you will be first-string. You're both important to the team, though, so don't get nervous. There will be plenty of play time for both of you. After laps and warm-up, you'll each run a few plays."

As the week progressed, Coach Yancy continued to watch Ryan and Chett. Ryan realized that Chett was more competition than he had originally thought. As far as Ryan could tell, they were about even. Both could pass well, but Chett had a better completion on the longer passes. Ryan, on the other hand, was fast on his feet and could run the ball better.

At the end of practice on Friday, Coach Yancy posted the team roster, showing who had made which position. Ryan looked for his name under quarterback. First-string: Chett Wilson. Second-string: Ryan Chapman. Ryan couldn't believe his eyes. *How could the coach place him as second-string? He was better than that.* Furious, he stormed out of the locker room.

When he arrived home, Lacy was watching a rerun on TV. "How'd it go?" she asked, knowing that today was the day the positions were to be posted.

"Don't ask," Ryan said.

"You didn't get it?" Lacy cried out and then regained her composure. "Well, don't let it get you down. It's only football. It's not the end of the world, you know."

Ryan didn't say anything, but went to his room to get ready for his date with Theresa. As the evening wore on, Ryan's foul mood persisted.

Finally losing patience, Theresa said, "Ryan, will you just get over yourself? You haven't even noticed my new outfit or asked me about my first week of school. You're so obsessed with this football thing. Maybe you should just take me home."

Over the next week, things didn't improve. Ryan continued to sulk. He considered quitting the team and tried to think of a way to sabotage Chett and even get revenge on Coach Yancy. He couldn't believe this was happening to him. During practice, Ryan spent most of his time on the sidelines while Coach Yancy worked with Chett on plays. He felt like a second-class citizen at school. His friends didn't say anything directly, but Ryan could tell they were talking about him getting passed over for quarterback.

Even Theresa seemed to avoid him. She no longer waited for him before school or sat with him at lunch. Finally, on Friday right before their first game of the year, she came clean, "Um, Ryan, I don't think this is going to work. I think we should see other people."

"Why?" he asked in disbelief.

"I just want to be free to see other people my senior year," she responded innocently.

Ryan didn't buy it. He and Theresa had already planned their senior year. He was supposed to be quarterback, and she was supposed to be homecoming queen. They had already talked about the prom and senior trip. They had reveled in the fact that they were going to be the most popular couple their senior year.

After the game that night, he saw Theresa talking to Chett Wilson and knew the truth. Theresa wanted to be part of a popular couple, and Ryan was no longer in the running. Second-string quarterback didn't cut it.

After the game, Ryan found Lacy on the living room floor surrounded by bits of paper, scissors, glue, and markers.

"Hey, you were great tonight," Lacy encouraged.

"Yeah, right. I only played half a quarter. Chett's the real winner."

"Well, you were good too. By the way, don't you have a date with Miss Supermodel tonight?"

"No, she dumped me too," Ryan admitted, beaten. His perfect senior year was not turning out the way he'd planned.

"Well, thank God," Lacy teased. "Now, you can live down here with the rest of us mere mortals. You've had a serious reality check, and I'm glad. You were thinkin' you were all that and more. I'm glad to have my brother back."

When he walked into the kitchen, he found a banner draped over the doorway

TRUTH UNPLUGGED:

A humble heart focuses on things that matter most and causes your steps to be sure.

that read You'll Always Be First-String to Me. Ryan laughed and grabbed his sister in a headlock. Lacy squealed, trying to escape.

"Tell the truth," Lacy said when Ryan finally let her go and she caught her breath, "aren't you relieved that you don't have someone concerned about whether or not your clothes clash with hers for the day? And just think: now you can play football for fun. There's no pressure. It's all on Chett."

Ryan thought about what Lacy had said. Although he wasn't entirely convinced that things were better, he had to admit that she had a point. Maybe his senior year wasn't going to be such a disaster after all.

TRUTH LINK:

Dear Lord, I want to stay humble no matter what goes right or wrong in my life. I don't want to get caught up in superficial things, and I really don't want to base my self-worth or how I value others on temporary things like looks, things, or position. Help me to keep pride out of my life. Amen.

POWER UP:

Pride is a dangerous thing. It sets you up for a fall without any warning. One minute you think you've got it all together; and the next minute, you're flat on your back, wondering what happened. And worse than that, pride alienates you from people who care about you. When you fall, you're alone.

Don't think your value or the value of others comes from accomplishments, looks, or superficial things. God values each of us because of who we are to Him, and He wants us to value each other for the same reason. When you recognize that your value comes from Him, pride will no longer have a hold on you.

BLINDSIDED

Rejection

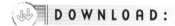 **DOWNLOAD:**

You are the ones chosen by God, chosen for the high calling of priestly work, chosen to be a holy people, God's instruments to do His work and speak out for him, to tell others of the night-and-day difference he made for you—from nothing to something, from rejected to accepted. 1 Peter 2:9-10

I think I'm gonna be sick, Patrick thought. For days, he had planned how he would ask Kristin out, and today was the day.

Although he had known *of* her since ninth grade, he hadn't really gotten to know her until a few weeks ago. They had met at a friend's birthday party. She was the editor of the school newspaper, and he loved photography. They talked for quite a while. Since then he had seen her in the halls and became anxious for the next edition of the school newspaper, so he could read her column. He had read the newspaper before, but had never noticed her column or how funny she was in it.

"Hey Kristin," he said, trying desperately to appear confident and smooth. "Loved your column this week."

"Oh, hi Patrick, thanks," she replied, stuffing books and folders into her backpack between classes.

"I was wondering, would you like to go play putt-putt at Snaggle's Family Center this Friday night?" he asked, his heart pounding.

Stopping her packing, she seemed to consider his question, "Oh, um, sure, that'd be fun," she said.

"Great. I'll pick you up at seven," he said. Inside he was doing cartwheels and screaming, *Yes!*

When he ran into his friend Nate, Patrick shared his good news. Nate and his girlfriend, Trista, had been a couple for a while, and Patrick trusted him for advice on ways to make the date a success. Nate congratulated him and gave him a few ideas for the evening: how to dress, budget, and other tips.

Patrick wanted to make a good impression, so he listened carefully to everything Nate said. In his mind, he was one step closer to having Kristin as his first girlfriend. He really liked her. She was pretty, smart, and funny.

On Friday night, Patrick had the entire night planned. He arrived at her house with a rose in hand. First, they enjoyed a casual dinner at the local diner. When the conversation began to lag, Patrick decided it was time to get going. They went to Snaggle's Family Center for putt-putt. Not wanting the evening to end too quickly, Patrick paid for two games of miniature golf.

Later that night, after dropping Kristin off, Patrick drove home feeling very pleased with the evening. It had gone just as he had planned. *I wonder what I can do for a follow-up,* he thought as he drove home. In fact, he spent the rest of the weekend thinking about it.

On Monday, he saw Kristin in the hallway between classes and waved. He thought she had seen him, but instead of waving back, she turned to go into the girls' restroom. During lunch he saw her again, but just before he got to her table, she left and headed in the opposite direction. After school, he went by her locker. She was there with one of her friends.

"Hey Kristin," he said.

"Oh, hi Patrick," she said slowly.

"I had a really good time on Friday," he said. "Maybe we could do it again."

Kristin closed her locker, hesitated a minute, and then said, "Patrick, you're a nice guy, but I just don't like you that way. I never did. We're just not right for each other."

Dumbstruck, Patrick watched her leave. For the life of him, he couldn't think of a reason why she had turned him down. *What went wrong?* he wondered.

 **TRUTH UNPLUGGED:**

Don't take rejection to heart. Instead, focus on how much God loves you. You really matter to Him.

For the rest of the day, Patrick felt numb. He couldn't believe Kristin didn't want to go out with him again when their date had gone so well. He had planned the entire thing, right down to the last penny.

Later he ran into Nate, who greeted him, "Hey! How's it going? How was your date with Kristin?"

Patrick shrugged. "I thought we had a good time, but when I asked her about going out again, she turned me down. She said she just didn't like me that way. I feel like such an idiot. I thought we would start dating, and, well, I guess that's not gonna happen."

Nate listened and then slapped Patrick on the back. "Patrick, you're a great guy. You're smart and funny and according to Trista, 'not bad looking.' Don't let one date, or one rejection, make you doubt yourself. You'll find a girl you click with, and the rest will be history."

"You think?" Patrick asked.

"I know. Trista says you'd be a great catch, and she has actually wanted to fix you up with a couple of her friends. If you want, I'll see who she has in mind, and maybe we can go on a double date," he said as they walked down the hall.

"I don't know that I want to put myself out there again, ya know?" Patrick said.

Nate stopped. "You can't let one rejection stop you from dating. So Kristin doesn't feel that way about you. How do you know that the next girl you ask out won't fall head over heels for you? Don't let Kristin's rejection keep you from making friends and meeting girls."

For a couple of days, Patrick thought about what Nate had said and decided that Nate was right—he couldn't let one disappointment get him down. On Thursday, he called Nate.

"Hey Nate, is the offer still open for Trista to fix me up for a double date?" he asked.

Nate replied happily, "As a matter of fact, I was just gonna call you about it. The carnival is in town on Saturday, and Trista has a friend who'd like to meet you. Her name is Nina, and she's really nice—pretty and fun too. I think you're gonna like her. How about we pick you up on Saturday at 6:30?"

"Okay, sounds good," Patrick said as his mom called him to dinner. *Maybe I'll give this dating thing another chance,* he thought as he hung up. *Nina—hmm—that's a pretty name . . .*

TRUTH LINK:

Dear Lord, I'm struggling with rejection. Someone I care about doesn't care about me. Help me to work through this and not to let it affect how I see myself. And help me not to keep other people at a distance because I'm afraid of getting hurt again. I want to be free to love people without living in fear of what they'll think of me or how they may treat me. Amen.

POWER UP:

Rejection is difficult to face. It can leave you doubting yourself and questioning your importance. Whether it's someone you like who doesn't like you back or a person who has refused your friendship, rejection hurts. If you're not careful, you'll begin to believe you're not worthy of that person's affection or friendship.

Don't harden your heart to keep others from getting close to you. You're valuable, just as you are, and you **WILL** meet people who will appreciate the qualities God has placed in you. Everyone faces rejection at some point, regardless of how smart, attractive, popular, or talented that person is. So remember, if you find yourself being rejected by someone, it's just one person's opinion. And another person's opinion does **NOT** define you.

NOT THE END OF THE WORLD

Peace

José stared down at his returned chemistry test. He couldn't believe it—a D minus. He'd studied for days. His throat constricted, and his stomach clenched. *What will this do to my grade?* he wondered in horror.

In all his years, he'd never received a D, not even on a homework assignment or pop quiz. He was an A student who had the potential to become the valedictorian during his senior year. Unlike many of his peers, he took his schoolwork seriously. He never blew it off. If anything, he went overboard. Last year, his algebra teacher had urged him to "relax and enjoy school," but he couldn't.

His parents had high hopes for him, often saying, "José, you can do anything you set your mind to, but you have to study. You won't get anywhere without a good education." His parents weren't wealthy by any means, but what they did have, they gave to him. "You are the hope of our family's future," they had said several times. José knew they would do anything to ensure that he received the best education. He felt responsible to give school his all—nothing less than 110 percent.

That's why he spent his afternoons and weekends pouring over his books and notes. And he chose only extracurricular activities that looked good on a college application. In fact, he spent most of his free time thinking of ways to improve his standing. While many students fulfilled their college entrance requirements and then took frivolous classes, José wouldn't even dream of it. He filled his schedule with the hardest honors classes and then pushed himself to pull an A every time.

"Are you okay, José?" his friend Juanita asked. "You look sick."

Speechless, José showed Juanita his paper.

"Oh, no!" Juanita gasped. "José, I'm so sorry. What happened?"

Unable to talk, he shrugged.

"Why don't you talk to Mr. Hernandez after class? Maybe there's been some mistake," she said, trying to console him.

After class, José approached Mr. Hernandez's desk, feeling defeated. "Mr. Hernandez, can I talk to you a minute?" he said as evenly as possible.

"José, I thought you might want to speak with me. I suppose you're shocked by the grade you received. Honestly, I was a bit surprised too. Did you not understand the material?"

José struggled to swallow the lump in his throat, "I thought I did. I don't know what happened." Then placing his test on Mr. Hernandez's desk, he asked, "Can you tell me what I did wrong?"

"Well, look here," Mr. Hernandez said, turning the test over. "You answered the first part of the essay question on quantum numbers and some of the second part, but you didn't answer the third part. That question was 50 percent of the grade."

José looked at the test again. Mr. Hernandez was right. He'd overlooked the third part of the question. He must have rushed and missed it. "What does this mean for my overall grade?" he asked.

"Let's see. You had an A going into this test. Now you're average is a high C. With the next test, you could still bring it up to a high B," he said.

José couldn't believe it. He'd never received anything less than an A. "So there's no way I can make an A now?" he asked in horror.

Mr. Hernandez looked compassionately at him. "I don't think it's likely. You may get close, but I doubt it."

Crushed, José quickly left Mr. Hernandez's room and rushed outside to get some fresh air. *How can I tell my parents? How could I let this happen?* he wondered. Unable to concentrate, José missed his next class and called his mother to come pick him up from school. When his mother finally arrived, José jumped into the car. Though José hadn't told his mother what had happened, he had conveyed that something was terribly wrong.

"José, what has you so upset? I've never seen you like this before," his mother asked concerned. José struggled to answer, but couldn't find the words. Instead, he pulled the test out of his bag and handed it to his mother. After looking at it a moment, his mother responded, "Oh José." Then pulling him into a hug, she comforted him. "It's okay. Everything is going to be okay. Did you talk to your teacher? Do I need to talk to him?"

Speaking for the first time, José responded, "No, I already talked to him. I messed up on the essay question." Then he confessed the worse part, "Mom, he said I can only make a B in the class now."

"It's okay, honey. We'll talk to your dad and work everything out. And if you get a B, then that'll be okay. It's not the end of the world," his mother comforted.

Later that evening, José's father came home. His parents talked in hushed tones in the kitchen while they prepared dinner. Then at dinner, his father asked, "How are you doing, José? Your mother told me what happened with your test and your grade."

José nodded, pushing his food around on his plate. "I'm so sorry, Dad. I messed up on the essay question. I knew the answer, but I forgot to finish it."

"Well, I'm sorry about your grade. It's a shame because I know you could earn an A, but really, I'm more concerned about you. You seem to be taking this

TRUTH UNPLUGGED:

God's peace can help you walk through any situation.

very hard, and I'm worried that we've pushed you too hard," he said, looking to his wife for affirmation.

José didn't know how to respond. He'd always been an A student. It's what he'd always been, and he knew it was what his parents expected. To him, there was never an option of anything other than an A.

"Your mother and I have talked about it, and we do want you to do your best. That makes us proud. But if your best is a B, that's okay too. We don't want you to expect perfection of yourself every time. Everyone makes mistakes. You just have to learn from them and move on," he continued.

José listened to his father but didn't understand exactly what he was talking about. He was an A student. He didn't get Bs. He couldn't just switch gears and start believing Bs were okay.

After dinner, he and his parents gathered in the living room for family devotions. They read from the Bible and then prayed.

It was something they tried to do every night. It was José's turn to read. In Matthew 26, he read that Jesus warned Peter that he would deny Him three times before the rooster crowed. Peter said he would never do that. Then at the end of the chapter, he did.

When José finished reading, he believed he kind of understood Peter's distress. Peter had made a mistake that he regretted deeply. Though José didn't compare his lapse on the chemistry exam to Peter's denial of the Lord, he did understand how difficult it was to live with a mistake. He also realized that Peter had gone on to be used by God, so his mistake wasn't the end of the story.

As he prayed that night, José asked God to give him wisdom about what had happened and to help him not to make the same mistake again. He also asked God for peace for the rest of the grading period, knowing that he probably wouldn't be able to redeem his grade. He had to live with his mistake. Truthfully, it might cost him the position of valedictorian, something he had worked for years to achieve, but he knew that with God's help, he would be okay.

As the days passed, he began to understand what his father had meant at dinner that night. Yes, José should always do his best. But sometimes that might not produce the results he hoped for. Of course he should enjoy the successes, but he would just have to let go of everything else.

TRUTH LINK:

Dear Lord, please show me how to have Your peace in my life. When I face difficult situations—even ones that are my fault—I pray that You'll help me to deal with them in peace. I don't want to live in turmoil over things I can't change, and I need Your help to accomplish that. Amen.

POWER UP:

Everyone faces challenges—expectations that are difficult to fulfill, disappointments, or mistakes. Even when those challenges come, you can still have peace in your life. You don't have to let worry, anger, fear, or discouragement overwhelm you. Instead, you can pray for God's peace to be with you, and you can remind yourself that He hasn't left you to deal with things on your own. He is there to help you find answers and to give you peace as you work through situations.

THE FALL GUY

Forgiveness

DOWNLOAD:

Be even-tempered, content with second place, quick to forgive an offense. Forgive as quickly and completely as the Master forgave you. Colossians 3:13

Toby saw Jarod sitting with a group of friends at the far corner of the cafeteria. Nervous, he walked their way. He wondered what Jarod would say to him. Until last week, they had been best friends. Everyone knew them as the daring duo—always thinking up crazy, funny things to do. Usually they conspired on harmless shenanigans—that is, until last week.

Last Wednesday, someone had vandalized Coach Dawson's office, riffling through it and toilet papering everything in sight. Chairs, tables, pictures, and more were turned upside down, with confetti and silly string piled high.

Coach Dawson *was* an easy target. Ask any student, and they would tell you that the coach was in a perpetual bad mood. The day of the incident, he had forced one class to run laps for an entire class period because a class clown had talked back to him. By the end of the class, students were close to passing out on the hot field.

Unfortunately, Toby had been that clown. He had meant his comment as a joke, but Coach Dawson had been in an especially foul mood. After class, Toby received angry comments from several students in class. He was on everyone's hit list.

When Jarod's school jacket was found in Coach Dawson's office, no one doubted that Jarod had committed the offense. Everyone knew Jarod and Toby were tight, and they assumed that Jarod had trashed the office out of revenge for Toby and to get back at Coach Dawson.

Jarod denied the incident, but unfortunately, that only made him appear even more guilty. Coach Dawson and the principal called his parents, suspended him for two days, enrolled him in detention for two weeks, and forced his parents to pay for the damage. According to Coach Dawson and the principal, Jarod got off easy. This sort of violation could have been turned over to the police and become a permanent mark on his record, affecting his college admissions.

As Toby approached the lunch table, the guys slid down to make room for him. They were in the middle of discussing the incident and Jarod's punishment.

"Man, I can't believe you're able to come back to school. Remember Jack Werner last year? He vandalized the art room, and they kicked him out of school for good," one guy said.

"They wanted to kick me out, but my dad talked them out of it by promising to pay for all the damage and having me do community service here at the school for the rest of the year," Jarod responded disgustedly.

"So who do you think did it? Coach Dawson had ticked everyone off by making the whole class run," another stated.

Jarod looked around the group, his gaze falling on Toby. "I can't say who did it. All I know is that it wasn't me."

Toby remained quiet during the discussion. Then unable to stand Jarod's scrutiny, he excused himself from the table.

After school, Toby braced himself as Jarod approached him in the parking lot. "Why'd you let me take the fall for that stunt, Toby? I know it had to have been you because you borrowed my jacket earlier that day."

Toby shifted uneasily. "I'm sorry, Jarod. I didn't mean for you to get in trouble. I left your jacket by accident. I was just mad that Coach Dawson made us run for the whole class. Everyone was mad at me, and I just wanted to get back at him."

Jarod scowled, "So why didn't you come forward when you knew they'd accused me?"

"Can you imagine what my dad would have done to me if he'd found out? He would've freaked—probably even sent me to military school or something," Toby desperately explained.

"Yeah, he probably would have said the same things that mine did. Do you realize that I am on restriction for the rest of the school year? And this summer, my parents are making me work for them for free just to pay them back? So basically, this stunt of yours has cost me the next six months of my life." Not waiting for an answer, Jarod stormed off.

Toby felt sick. Everything had gotten way out of hand. He had only meant to get even with Coach Dawson. He hadn't meant for Jarod to take the fall, but what could he do? If he spoke up now, everyone would hate him for not speaking up sooner. And *his* dad would ground him for life, he was certain.

Several weeks following the incident, Toby didn't see Jarod much. Jarod was either in class, in detention, or picking up trash around the school. Toby began to stay after school to help Jarod pick up the trash. He tried desperately to make it up to his friend. Although Jarod thanked him for the help, they didn't speak much as they worked.

During lunch, their gang of friends continued to sit together. Toby wanted everything to go back to the way it had been before the vandalism, with Jarod and him hanging out and joking around together. It took quite a while, but slowly things seemed to return to normal.

One day after school, Toby approached Jarod. "Hey Jarod, do you want to go grab a burger? I'm starving."

Jarod looked away, "I wish I could, but I can't. See ya."

As Jarod started to walk away, Toby stopped him, "Are you gonna hold this against me forever? I said I was sorry."

TRUTH UNPLUGGED:

Forgiveness sets you free from the very thing causing the hurt.

Jarod turned toward him, "Look, I've forgiven you. It's just that I'm still on restriction. I can't hang out after school."

"Will you be able to hang out this summer? Maybe come swimming at my house?" Toby asked.

Before Toby left, Jarod promised to ask his dad. He was set to work all summer, but maybe his dad would ease up on the restrictions.

As Toby watched Jarod leave, he felt sick. Jarod had forgiven him even when he hadn't deserved it. As he headed for home, he felt ashamed. Jarod was a better friend to Toby than Toby had been to Jarod. It was something Toby decided to change.

I need to talk to Dad when I get home, Toby thought. Then he made plans to confess and face the punishment for vandalizing Coach Dawson's office, like he should have done months ago.

TRUTH LINK:

Dear Lord, please help me forgive those who have hurt or offended me. I realize I need to forgive them, but I need Your help. I need to know how to forgive them once and for all, and I also need to know how to handle myself around them in the future. Amen.

POWER UP:

Have you had a difficult time forgiving someone who has hurt or offended you? You may think, **BUT YOU DON'T KNOW WHAT THEY DID. THEY DON'T DESERVE TO BE FORGIVEN.** And you're probably right. They probably don't deserve forgiveness, but forgiveness isn't to benefit them; it's for you. As you forgive, you free yourself from the pain and bitterness. You become free to care for others instead of living in fear of being hurt again. You become free from being held captive by that sickening feeling that hits you whenever you see that person.

It may take time, but make the decision to forgive and continue to make that decision whenever painful memories come to mind. In time, the memories won't be painful. At that point, you'll know you're free. What a great feeling that will be!

THE RIGHT PLACE FOR NOW

Decision-making

DOWNLOAD:

I choose the true road to Somewhere, I post your road signs
at every curve and corner. Psalm 119:30

Gregory watched his mother rush through the coffee-house
doors. Moving forward in long swift strides, she came toward him
and hastily removed her overcoat. "Hey there. Sorry I'm late. I got
held up at the store," she said. Throwing her long burgundy wool
coat over a nearby chair, she flopped down and reached for her
cappuccino. "Thanks for ordering for me. I've been looking forward
to this all day," she said as she took a sip of the creamy hot drink.

Gregory smiled weakly. *She looks tired,* he thought to himself.
These days, she always looks tired.

"Okay, let's see," she said. "Where are those applications?"

Out of his backpack, Gregory carefully pulled a manila folder
that contained a handful of college applications. *How can I tell
her?* he wondered as he handed her the folder. *She's gonna freak.*

Since the accident, Gregory's mother had struggled to help him navigate through his senior year. Four months ago, his father had been killed in a traffic accident on his way home from work. Gregory watched his mother try to stay positive, but he could see that she was so fragile on the inside. He knew his father's death had devastated her, although she tried to put on a brave face. With his upcoming high school graduation, college in the fall, dealing with his father's insurance company, funeral bills, and her flower shop to keep running, he knew she was doing her best to keep her head above water.

"So, is Dartmouth your first choice? Or are you thinking Cornell?" she said lightheartedly as she reached for the stack of applications.

Gregory watched her. "What're you gonna do, Mom?"

"What do you mean, what am I gonna do? I'm going to help you fill these out."

"No, I mean what are you gonna do when I leave for college?" he asked carefully.

"Well, honey, I'm going to miss you. But you'll be home for the holidays. And your brother is still at home with me. And I have work. People will still need flowers," she joked. Then she softly added, "I'll get by. I'll miss you, but I'll get by."

A long silence followed until she added, "Just promise me you'll come home at Christmas. Don't go falling head over heels for some girl and forget about me. I figure I have a few more years before I have to relinquish my position as the main woman in your life."

He gave her a small grin and shifted his attention to the applications she held. "Okay, let's get started," he said.

"Well, let's see. How about starting with the big boys? We've got Dartmouth, Cornell, and Brown. Which one should we talk about first?"

"Actually, Mom, I think I want to start with Baylor," he said, broaching the subject he had wanted to talk to her about for weeks.

His mother stopped shuffling through the papers and looked at him in surprise. Baylor was her alma mater—and his father's.

"Baylor?" she asked in disbelief.

"Yeah, it's a great school, and it's got a good pre-med program," he said.

Hesitating, his mother said, "I know it's a great school. I went there. But honey, you have never mentioned Baylor before. I don't want you to make a decision like this because of your dad's death. I want you to do what's best for you. Your father would want you to do what's best for you too."

"Mom, look. I've been thinking about it a lot lately. Actually, it had crossed my mind before Dad died. And now—well, now I want to apply there. Coach Turner is an alumnus, too, and I've asked him about it. I even visited the campus last week after school and talked to a counselor. I'm sure I'd get accepted—maybe even get a good scholarship. Anyway, it's where I want to start."

TRUTH UNPLUGGED:

Let God help you make big and small decisions in your life. He knows what's best for you.

Gregory knew his parents had dreamed and planned for him to attend a top East Coast school. They had sent him to the best college-prep school in the area, hired tutors, enrolled him in athletics and music programs, and struggled to save enough money to pay for it all. They joined community groups, built homes for the poor, took him to Central America with their church to give medical aid to the needy—anything to give him a well-rounded education. He knew the thought of him going to a local school—even a good one—would be hard for her to take, but with his father's death, he couldn't leave—not yet.

"But, Gregory, we've planned this. You've wanted to go to an East Coast school since the fifth grade. And now what? You want to throw all that away? All the plans, all the hard work?" his mother's voice strained.

"Mom . . . " Gregory hesitated and then leveled his eyes on hers, "I'm just not ready to leave yet."

"You can't be scared to leave home."

"I'm not scared. I'm concerned about you."

"What do you mean 'concerned'? Honey, I'm fine."

Gregory scooted forward in his seat and leaned toward his mother. "Mom, I see you. I watch you work so hard to make everything okay. I hear you cry sometimes at night. I know you miss Dad. I know you feel alone. I just *can't* leave."

"Gregory, listen to me. I know things have been difficult, but I'm going to be fine."

"You're right, Mom. You're gonna be fine. But right now, you need me. And so does Justin. I can't leave him without a father *and* a big brother in the same year. And I need you guys too."

"But this is *your* time. You shouldn't be concerned about anything else. Don't stay behind because of us."

"I don't think of it as staying behind. I still want to study pre-med; I just don't want to go halfway around the world to do it. I can't go halfway around the world right now. Not right now.

His mother watched him as a tear slid down her face.

Gregory sat back, looking around, "Geez, Mom, don't cry. This isn't a bad thing."

"Oh, I'm not sad," she said, reaching out to wrap her hand around the warm cappuccino sitting on the table, "I'm just proud of you. And your dad would have been proud of you too." Regaining her composure, she said, "Okay, if you're sure Baylor is your top choice, we'll work on it first."

For the next two hours, they worked their way through the applications, discussing each entrance essay in detail. As they looked over the applications and discussed the instruction to "Describe an event that has shaped your life," Gregory reflected over the last several months. Before, he probably would have talked about his trip to Central America or winning an important basketball game, but his father's death had changed that. He marveled at how quickly life could change. And though he definitely wouldn't have chosen it, he knew that he would appreciate life more now, because he had a deeper understanding of how quickly it could end.

He hoped his father would have understood his decision to stay close to home for college. Though, when he thought of how much his father had taught him about the importance of family—especially as he remembered how much his father had done for him—he knew his father would have. In some ways, Gregory knew he was taking up a leadership role in his family by helping his mother and staying accessible for his little brother, but he was confident that it was what he needed to do. Life could change quickly, and he didn't want to waste a moment of it being in the wrong place.

TRUTH LINK:

Dear Lord, as I make choices in my life—how I will live, where I will go, and what I will do—I pray that I'll make decisions that are pleasing to You. Please help me to follow the path You have planned for me. Amen.

POWER UP:

Throughout your life, you'll have many decisions to make. You'll decide what education you'll receive, what profession you'll pursue, who you'll marry, where you'll live, and more. As you make each decision—big or small—always look to God to show you the best choice. Through scripture and prayer, you can know His will for your life. You may even discover that something you have already decided—a choice that seems like a no-brainer—needs reconsideration because He has something so much better in store.

THE BEST BIRTHDAY PRESENT EVER

Love

DOWNLOAD:

Be devoted to one another in brotherly love. Honor one another above yourselves. Romans 12:10 NIV

"I know what I want for my birthday," Shannon proclaimed. Her golden curls danced around her eight-year-old head.

"Oh, yeah? What?" Stephen asked as they walked out the front door for school.

Stephen dropped Shannon off at her elementary school each morning on his way to the high school. Shannon admitted she felt so cool having her big brother drop her off instead of her parents. Stephen didn't mind. He loved his little sister and found her amusing. Shannon was by far his biggest fan.

"I wanna go to the Tween Jam concert next month," Shannon announced. "It'd be my first concert."

Cautiously, Stephen asked, "Who do you want to take with you?"

"You, silly. It'll be so cool for us to go together," she said emphatically.

Stephen smiled nervously. There was no way he could be seen at a Tween Jam concert. The concert tour catered to kids under the age of twelve. Stephen was certain he would die of embarrassment if anyone ever found out that he had gone, let alone if anyone saw him there. Oh, no, it wasn't going to happen.

"Shannon, maybe you should think of something else for your birthday," he ventured.

Shannon gazed at him with her big, brown eyes. "Why?" she asked innocently.

"I just think you could come up with something even better," Stephen offered.

TRUTH UNPLUGGED:

Show the love of God by putting others first.

After a few minutes of silence, Shannon turned to Stephen. "I've thought about it, and I wanna go to the Tween Jam concert with you," she said, nodding her head in excitement. "You said I could pick *anything* under thirty dollars, and this would be. And I think we can have the *coolest* time ever."

Unable to think of a quick response, Stephen remained quiet. *Oh Lord, get me outta this. It'd be so embarrassing,* he thought.

Over the next month, Stephen tried to subtlety convince Shannon to pick another birthday present. He did *not* want to be the only teenager at the concert surrounded by five hundred screaming, little pop princess wannabes. But no matter what he said, he couldn't dissuade her. Shannon just said over and over again that they would be the coolest brother and sister at the concert. There was no getting out of it.

On the night of the concert, Shannon jabbered nonstop. She had proudly told everyone she knew that she was going to the

Tween Jam concert with her big brother. Stephen groaned inwardly, *Now, everyone knows.*

Inside the arena, they found their seats: fourth row, center. To make matters worse, the three rows in front of them and the seats around them were mostly empty. So there was no hiding in the crowd. Stephen felt like he was on display.

As each band played, Shannon jumped, clapped, screamed, and danced until she glistened with sweat. "Come on, Stephen," she urged, trying to pull him to his feet. "Stand up with me."

Stephen nervously looked around. Other than parents, he was the only person over twelve in the place. "No, Shannon, I just want to watch."

During intermission, Stephen had no choice but to take Shannon to get autographs and refreshments. As they stood in line, Shannon was quiet.

"Hey," Stephen nudged, "aren't you having fun?"

"Yeah, I just wish you were more fun. I thought it would be so cool to come with you, but you just sit there. You're not yelling or clapping or anything."

"Sorry. This is just kind of a little kid thing," Stephen said.

"But it's *my* birthday present," Shannon pleaded, looking up at Stephen.

Stephen felt ashamed. Suddenly, he saw the event through his sister's eyes. He saw how important the concert was to her. He realized how important it was for his biggest fan to go to her first concert with her big brother. He had allowed what others might think of him to keep him from giving his little sister a great birthday. Shannon deserved better than that.

"I'm sorry, Shannon. I should get into the spirit of things more. I tell you what, why don't we make the rest of the night the best ever?"

"How?" Shannon asked.

Looking around, Stephen came up with a plan. "To start with, you stay here and get the autographs from this band, and I'll go over there, so I can get the autographs from the opening band. That way we'll get both before the second half of the concert starts."

"You mean it?" Shannon asked, wide-eyed.

"Of course. Just stay where I can see you and don't talk to anyone. As soon as you finish, stand at the end of the signing table and wait until I get there. Then don't move, okay?"

Shannon agreed, and Stephen was off.

For the rest of the night, they sang, screamed, clapped, and jumped up and down until they were exhausted. Stephen had to admit he had a good time once he quit thinking about who might see him and focused on his little sister.

On the way home, Shannon and Stephen sang all the Tween Jam songs at the top of their lungs. Shannon bounced in her seat and proclaimed the night was "the best of my whole life."

Stephen laughed, "Ya know, I think it's right up there for me too." He knew he would never forget taking his little sister to her first concert and giving her the best birthday present ever.

 ## TRUTH LINK:

Dear Lord, I want to be someone who shows love and kindness to others. Help me not to be held back because of the fear of what others might think. Instead show me how to put others first every day so that I can be an example of Your love. Amen.

 ## POWER UP:

It's hard to continually put others first. At times, it can be very uncomfortable, but as you do, you communicate their importance. You show how valuable they are, and you become an ambassador of God's love to the world.

THE DOUBLE LIFE

church

DOWNLOAD:

Let us not give up meeting together, as some are in the habit of doing, but let us encourage one another. Hebrews 10: 25 NIV

"Hey Duncan, it's David. You want me to come get you for youth group?"

"Nah, man. I'm skippin' tonight. I'm going over to Joel's," Duncan explained.

Silence.

"That makes the third week you've missed youth group, and you haven't made it to church for the last two Sundays either. What's up?" David asked with concern.

"Nothing. I just don't feel like going to youth group or church," Duncan said flatly. He'd attended church all of his life, but since his dad started working on Sundays, he didn't have to go.

"Sounds to me like you're starting a bad habit," David countered. "You know Joel isn't the kind of guy you need to take cues from. Don't get me wrong, he's fun, but he parties and runs with a pretty rough crowd."

Duncan expected this from David. David was at church every time the doors were open. Though Duncan and he used to hang out a lot, Duncan had decided that church wasn't as necessary as he'd once thought.

"You're just judging him, man. You don't even really know him. Besides, we don't party. We just hang out at his house and watch movies."

Again, silence.

"Say what you will. I'm still praying for you," David said simply.

Just as I thought. David's turning this into some superspiritual lecture. Why can't he just leave me alone, Duncan thought as they said good-bye and hung up the phone. He and David were friends, but he felt that David needed to lighten up. *Just because I don't want to go to church doesn't mean I'm not a Christian.*

Later that evening at Joel's, Duncan and Joel discussed Duncan's decision to blow off youth group.

"Man, you couldn't pay me to go to church," Joel said with disgust. "Bunch of Holy Rollers."

"It's not so bad," Duncan said, feeling a bit uneasy as Joel laughed at him. He wasn't used to having to defend his faith or his friends at church.

The next day, David called Duncan again. "Hey, we missed you last night. Lots of people asked about you. You know there's a lock-in planned for next Friday night during spring break? We're gonna have the whole church to ourselves with pizza and games and movies all night long. You should come."

Duncan promised to think about it. He wasn't sure what he wanted to do. He was having so much fun hanging out with Joel and his other new friends that he couldn't imagine giving up a Friday night to hang around church.

When he mentioned it to Joel later, Joel laughed again. "Are you seriously considering going?" he asked in shock. "Duncan, if you haven't figured it out yet, lemme tell ya, church is for losers. You don't want to go running around at some lame church all night, do you?"

Duncan felt torn. On one hand, he had David trying to get him to come back to church; and on the other hand, he had Joel telling him he'd be a loser if he did. Duncan didn't *hate* church. He just wanted to take a break from it for a while. He'd been almost every week of his life because his dad forced him to go. Now, he had to make up his own mind. He knew that, according to everything he'd been taught, Joel wasn't the best kind of friend to have; but on the other hand, Joel was fun.

On Thursday of spring break week, Duncan and Joel were hanging out with a few other new friends when Joel handed Duncan a flask. "Here, try this."

"What is it?" Duncan asked uneasily.

"Just a little pick-me-up. Trust me, you'll like it," Joel laughed.

Duncan took a sip. The liquid burned the back of his throat and continued all the way down. He coughed and sputtered. He felt like his insides were on fire. Everyone laughed.

"Told ya you'd like it," Joel nodded. "I took it from my parents' cabinet. Go on, have some more."

Though Duncan hadn't wanted to drink the alcohol, he didn't want the guys to think he couldn't take it. So for the rest of the evening, he drank with the rest of them. He didn't return home until the early morning hours. Since his dad was out of town on a business trip, Duncan stumbled his way through the dark, quiet house and finally collapsed in his bed.

As soon as he lay down, he felt the room spin. Nausea hit him. He knew he was going to vomit. Rushing to his bathroom, he made it just in time, but with each hurl, he felt another one coming. Wave after wave hit him as he crouched on the floor.

In the morning, he woke up on the bathroom floor to the sound of someone banging on the front door. Still feeling lousy, he opened the door. David stood there giving him a strange look.

"What happened to you?" he asked with concern.

"Nothing. I just woke up," he responded. Just then, he felt another wave of nausea hit him, and he ran. David followed him to the bathroom.

"Are you okay?" he asked. Then as if a light bulb flashed on, he said, "You've been drinking."

Coming up for air, Duncan scowled. "So what. Don't get all high and mighty on me."

David shook his head. "Yeah, I can see I'm the one with the problem here." Then going to the linen closet, he grabbed a washcloth and soaked it with cool water. "Here put this on your forehead."

TRUTH UNPLUGGED:

Don't think of attending church as an obligation. Instead, consider it an opportunity to grow in who you are in Christ and meet others who share your faith.

Taking a seat on the edge of the tub, David watched his friend. "Man, what are you doing? You are so much smarter than this."

"I just wanted to have some fun with my friends."

"Your friends, huh? If they're so great, why'd they get you drunk? And where are they now?"

"Don't preach at me. I really don't need it," Duncan said weakly. His head throbbed.

"Don't you get it, man? I care. I don't want you heading down this road." Then shaking his head he added, "I just came over here to see what you were gonna do today. That's all."

Over the next several hours, Duncan slowly started feeling better. He slept, ate, and finally felt well enough to watch TV on the couch. David stayed with him the entire time, just to make sure he was okay. Later that afternoon, as David started to leave for the lock-in, he asked Duncan one more time to come.

Duncan thought about it. He figured it was the least he could do since David had spent the entire day taking care of him, not to mention that pizza sounded really good. When he walked in the door, his old friends from youth group gave a shout, welcoming him back. As the evening wore on and the group played flashlight chase, had shaving cream fights, stuffed themselves on pizza, and watched movies, Duncan couldn't remember why he'd stayed away so long. He had a blast! It was as if he'd never left, and it was sure more fun than drinking and getting sick with Joel and his friends.

Duncan thought back to when Joel called his church friends losers. After the last twenty-four hours, Duncan knew without a doubt that his church friends weren't losers. They didn't have to party to have a good time, and that sounded pretty smart to him.

TRUTH LINK:

Dear Lord, I ask You to show me where to go to church. I know I need to be a part of a church body. I pray that You'll help me make good friends, too, so we can encourage one another in our faith and grow spiritually. Amen.

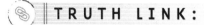 ## POWER UP:

There comes a time in every person's life when he or she has to decide whether or not to attend church. When you're young, your parents may take you, but as you get older, it becomes your choice. Don't think of church as an obligation; think of it as an opportunity to meet with great people who believe the same way you do. You'll find real friends who want what's best for you, instead of people who try to drag you down.

If you don't already attend church, take time to pray about where you should go. Pray that you'll find the right church and meet the right friends. Then allow Jesus to lead you to your church home. Soon you'll find a place of refuge where you can learn about God and make strong friends who will have a positive influence on you.

THE ACCIDENT

Trusting God

DOWNLOAD:

When I get really afraid I come to you in trust. I'm proud to praise God; fearless now, I trust in God. Psalm 56:3-4

As the bright summer sun climbed overhead, the temperature was rising. It was going to be a scorcher. After spending an exhilarating, yet tiring, morning running along the lake, Dean wanted to kick back and enjoy a small reward—a cold slushy—one of his favorite childhood drinks. As he stepped off the concrete curb, he heard the rattle of a speeding truck approaching. Turning, he realized it was too late . . .

Startled, Dean awoke. His heart raced, sweat poured from his brow, and his breath was ragged. The accident. He'd relived it almost every night for the last four months. After looking around, he remembered where he was—the rehabilitation clinic. Though the staff tried to make the room homey, Dean knew better. This wasn't his home. It wasn't even close. Looking down,

Dean saw the lumps, formerly known as his legs, resting life-lessly under the sheet.

Though time had passed, he still couldn't believe it. *Paralyzed.* The word just hung in the air. It all had happened so fast. One minute he had been enjoying a run along the lake, and the next he was in traction—cast-covered from head to toe.

He'd been unconscious for a few days following the accident. By the time he woke up, the heavy medication had dulled any pain. Now, he almost wished for the pain. At least then he could feel something—anything. Two weeks following the accident, the doctors gave him their prognosis—paralysis from the waist down.

At first, he denied their diagnosis. He thought for sure they'd made a mistake or had underestimated his ability to recover. Each day he woke up thinking that today would be the day he'd feel something—a pin prick, a chill from an overactive air conditioner, the softness of sheets—but that day never came.

He replayed the last few moments of his life as a walking person over and over in his mind. If only . . . If only he hadn't gone running at the lake. If only he hadn't stopped for an icy. If only he'd seen the truck sooner. If only . . .

He was still angry. Angry at the truck driver. Angry at anyone who tried to comfort him. Angry at everyone who took care of him. Angry at God.

In reality that was where most of his anger was directed—at God. God was supposed to take care of him. God's angels were supposed to protect him. God's Holy Spirit was supposed to warn him. Where had He been that morning?

Visitors tried to comfort Dean, but their words sounded hollow. They told him the accident "must have been God's will," but he couldn't think of any reason why being thrown in front of a truck would glorify God. Or they said that Dean "must have sinned and caused the accident." Dean was raised in a Christian home and had become a Christian at an early age. He tried to live right. He loved God, his family, his friends, and his church. He didn't cheat, steal, party, or curse. For the life of him, he couldn't think of anything he had done to invite this. One person had even tried to console him by saying, "When God closes a door, He opens a window." Right then, Dean wanted to push that person out of a window.

Now, he felt lethargic, like nothing mattered. He wanted to disappear or just not wake up in the morning—anything to keep from facing his present life. As he lay in his bed wishing he could just forget everything, Dean's therapist, Alfred Thomas, came into the room to get ready for his session. "Hey Dean, how are you today? Ready to get moving?" Alfred asked in his typically friendly way.

No matter what Dean said, Alfred's disposition never changed. He was always friendly and happy. Dean tried to dislike him, but from the beginning Alfred knew just what to say. He'd worked with many paraplegics to get them mobile again. He pushed Dean to exhaustion, demanding that he improve.

"Today I'd like to continue to work with you on strengthening your upper body," Alfred explained as he reviewed Dean's chart.

"I don't feel like working today," Dean said flatly.

Looking up from his notes, Alfred said, "Well, you know, the sooner we get you working, the sooner you can get back here to feel sorry for yourself."

"What do you know about it?" Dean glared at him.

Alfred set his notes aside. "Well, I know you have to make a choice. You can lay here and give in to depression, or you can move forward, learn to be mobile, and get on with your life."

"What life?"

"A life that may be different from what you've known, but it can still be fulfilling," Alfred said.

Down in the physical therapy room, Dean struggled to lift weights. Things that had once been easy now proved overwhelmingly difficult. Again, he remembered running for miles around the lake. Now, he had difficulty doing simple reps on a weight machine.

After his workout, Alfred took Dean outside for fresh air. Wheeling effortlessly around a basketball court, another young man in a wheelchair played basketball with some children who seemed to experience all sorts of physical challenges. Dean watched him play, smoothly swooshing back and forth. He could almost move as easily in his chair as walking people move on two legs. "Who's he?" Dean asked.

"Oh, that's Mike Conners. He's amazing, isn't he?" Alfred said as he wheeled Dean around the activity court. "You know, he's only been in that chair for a year."

"What happened to him?"

"Car accident. He was a lot like you," Alfred said. "He was young, active, and really into sports. He had a hard time at first, but he made it. He comes back each week for therapy and then stays to play basketball."

TRUTH UNPLUGGED:

When bad things happen, continue to trust God. Instead of wondering why something has happened, ask God to help you move forward. He can turn it around and bring great gain to something you might consider loss.

"So, he's my inspiration?" Dean asked sarcastically.

"Only if you want him to be. Everyone has to make his or her own choice about whether to move forward or not. No one can make that decision for you."

At the end of their walk, Dean asked Alfred to let him sit alone to enjoy the sun for a while. As he sat there, he looked around, watching the other patients. Some were sitting like him. Others were moving around the grounds, and still others were playing like Mike was, their faces flushed from the exercise.

Then Dean looked back over at Mike Connors. "He was a lot like you," Dean remembered Alfred saying. To Dean, that seemed unreal. Mike looked like he didn't have a care in the world. He moved in his chair with ease. Inside Dean decided, *I want to be like that. I want to enjoy life again.* But he knew he couldn't do it alone. He needed help.

Lord, I don't know why this happened to me, Dean prayed. *I'm not even sure it matters anymore. It happened, and whatever the reason, it doesn't seem worth it to be angry or depressed anymore. I'm only hurting myself. I want to move forward, but I need help. Please help me. I trust You with my future. I know You're the only One who can help me through this.*

It was the first time Dean had truly had a heart-to-heart with God in months. As he prayed, he knew that his outward circumstances hadn't changed; but inside, he felt a comfort that he had missed and hadn't felt in a long time. He felt a glimmer of hope begin to sparkle. He would continue to pray for God to help him walk again, but until that happened, he wouldn't sit still waiting. He'd start working—building his strength, searching for God's joy, and believing for God's will every day.

TRUTH LINK:

Dear Lord, I am facing a situation that I don't understand. I don't know why it has happened, but instead of letting myself fall into self-pity, I pray that You will show me how to move forward. I pray that You will show me how to pray, and I ask You to lead me to Scriptures that will encourage me as I read my Bible. I want to honor You, even in difficult times. Please show me how to do that. Amen.

POWER UP:

Have you ever wondered why bad things happen to good people? When terrible things happen, people usually wrestle with **WHY**. Why did God allow it? Why did it happen? They often get angry and depressed. The truth is, knowing why doesn't change the situation. You still have to trust God through it—trust Him to change the outcome, trust Him to help you through, and trust Him to show you how to face each day. That doesn't mean you just resign yourself to accept less than God's best, but it means you continue to move forward, trusting God and praying.

THE INTRUDER

Jealousy

DOWNLOAD:

Where jealousy and selfish ambition exist, there is disorder and every evil thing. But the wisdom from above is first pure, then peaceable, gentle, reasonable, full of mercy and good fruits, unwavering, without hypocrisy. And the seed whose fruit is righteousness is sown in peace by those who make peace.

James 3:16-18 NASB

"Run Jacob! Go for it!" Tony cheered from the sidelines as his best friend raced down the soccer field heading for the goal—his third for the day.

Tony and Jacob had been next-door neighbors and best friends for years. They'd grown up together. As toddlers, they played together in their playpens. In elementary school, they played soccer every afternoon, and during the summers, they'd lived at the public pool. These days, they spent hours playing video games, practicing soccer, and volunteering at church.

As the soccer game ended, Tony ran over to Jacob to congratulate him on scoring the winning goal. They gave each other a high five as the rest of their teammates jumped up and down. "Man, way to go," Tony said excitedly. "Three goals! You the man!"

"Thanks! Did you see that last one? That guy almost tripped me, but I caught myself and kept going. But boy, for a second, I thought I was gonna eat dirt," he said, with a victorious smile.

"Yeah, I did. Hey, do you want to try that new burger joint on Main Street? It's supposed to have awesome double cheeseburgers."

Jacob's smile faltered. "Oh, sorry Tony. I'm going to get something to eat with Tracy Guiness," Jacob said.

"Oh, okay. I'll see you later then," Tony said. He and Jacob had always grabbed burgers after their games, so Tony was confused and a little disappointed. Tracy was a new girl at school, and Jacob had a couple of classes with her. He'd mentioned her a few times, but Tony had never imagined they liked each other.

For the next few days, Tony couldn't get rid of the nagging feeling that Tracy was becoming a major obstacle in his friendship with Jacob. He noticed that Jacob had started hanging out with Tracy in between classes and after school. In the past, Jacob usually came over to play Nintendo after school, but now Tony rarely saw him. He tried to take it in stride, but he felt deserted. It wasn't that he disliked Tracy; in reality, he didn't even know her. But right now, it didn't matter. All Tony could see was that he had a lot more free time on his hands because his best friend was being led away by some girl.

The following week, Tony arrived early at youth group. He hadn't seen Jacob in several days and had hoped to catch up and play some air hockey before the group began. But Jacob didn't arrive until about five minutes before starting time, and Tracy was with him. Tony couldn't believe Jacob had brought *her* there. This was one of the activities the two guys enjoyed the most.

Jacob waved and motioned for Tony to join them, but Tony turned away, taking a seat at the back of the group with a few of the other guys. After the group dismissed, several people gathered for refreshments, including Tony. While Tracy was across the room talking to a girl she knew from school, Jacob came up behind Tony saying, "Hey there, why didn't you come sit with us? I wanted to introduce you to Tracy."

Tony glanced his way and then said coolly, "I already know who Tracy is. You don't have to introduce us." Tony knew he was being rude, but he couldn't help it. He didn't want Tracy to be there.

Jacob frowned, looking confused. Tony knew that Jacob was trying to figure out what was bothering him. *Whatever,* he thought.

"Well, do you want to go with us to get ice cream on the way home? A few others are going to join us too," he asked.

"Nah," Tony responded. "I wouldn't want to crash your date."

"It's not a date," Jacob said shortly. "I told you other people are coming too."

"Sorry," Tony said, "but I'm not interested." Then turning, he left.

Out in the parking lot, Tony got into his car and just sat there. He felt like he was on the verge of losing his best friend to some girl. It wasn't like they both hadn't had girlfriends in the past, but Tony could tell Tracy was different. Jacob could really fall for her. He looked up as the group exited the building and headed to the ice cream parlor. Several people, Jacob and Tracy included, walked and laughed their way to their cars. Tony watched them, feeling left out. He wanted to go, but unable to swallow his pride, he drove home.

Later that night, as he studied in his room, his phone rang. Answering it, he heard Jacob on the other end. "Hey man, what was up with you tonight? Why'd you blow me off like that? And why don't you like Tracy? What'd she ever do to you?" Jacob's questions came like rapid bullets from a machine gun.

"So I don't like your girlfriend," Tony shot back. "So what?"

"Yeah, well it's bugged me all night. My best friend blows me off and doesn't want to hang out with the girl I like. What's up with that?"

Tony's emotions ranged from contrite to angry. On one hand, he felt bad about acting like such a jerk, but on the other, he didn't care. Jacob deserved to get blown off just like Jacob had blown off Tony lately.

When Tony didn't respond, Jacob continued, "Oh, I get it; you're jealous. I have a girlfriend, and you don't. That's why you've been acting like this. Tracy never did anything to you. I thought you were bigger than that."

"I'm not jealous that you have a girlfriend, but I sure don't like you blowing me off every time she snaps her fingers," Tony shot back. "Like us not going to get burgers after the soccer games or hanging out after school. Man, I never see you anymore."

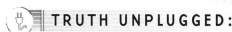 **TRUTH UNPLUGGED:**

Don't allow jealousy to poison your relationships and drive a wedge between you and your friends. Trust your friends' care for you, and trust God to orchestrate your friendships. He has your best interest at heart.

Jacob remained quiet for a few seconds before responding. "Man, I'm sorry, but Tracy and I are dating. I have to make time for her too. What do you say we all go out for burgers after next week's game? Or maybe you could invite a date, and we'll double. We just have to work something out. I don't want my best friend and my girlfriend to hate each other."

"I don't hate her," Tony said in frustration. "I'm just not used to having her around all the time. But I guess I could make an effort to get to know her."

"Yeah, she's really cool. You'll like her," Jacob encouraged.

After they hung up, Tony thought for quite a while about the situation. Jacob was the best friend he'd ever had, and unless he came to terms with Tracy, he could lose Jacob's friendship.

He took a few minutes to pray. He asked God to help him be more understanding and to help him not feel angry and left out when Jacob wanted to spend more time with Tracy. He also started thinking about other friends that he could hang out with so he didn't feel so alone.

After he'd come up with a game plan, he sat back and tried to figure out who he was going to ask out for his double date with Jacob and Tracy. Sandy Jones had been flirting with him lately in English class. *Hmm—Maybe she'd like to go . . .*

TRUTH LINK:

Dear Lord, please forgive me for becoming jealous and allowing strife to enter my friendship. I need Your help to know how to deal with what I'm feeling. Show me if my friendship is just changing or if I'm overreacting. Either way, help me to be secure in my relationships, to act with integrity, and to rely on You in everything I do. Amen.

POWER UP:

Jealousy is a dangerous element in friendship. It can end even the best of relationships. Before you know it, jealousy can make you begin to view every comment, look, and action with suspicion. Then strife enters the picture, and the relationship is one step closer to death. Instead of giving in to jealousy, ask God to show you how you can become more secure in your friendships.

It's not ever easy to lose a friendship, but friendships do change. At one point, you mean the world to each other, and then circumstances change and you find yourself hanging out with different people. It can be a difficult transition, but don't succumb to jealousy and strife. Whether the change is real or imagined, you must trust God to bring the right relationships into your life at the right time. He wants what's best for you all the time—even in your friendships.

THE UNEXPECTED HERO

Inner Strength

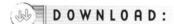

DOWNLOAD:

"Pray constantly that you will have the strength and wits to make it through everything that's coming and end up on your feet before the Son of Man." Luke 21:36

Josh dragged himself through the door after school, feeling thankful to be done with school for the week. Ugh! He hated school. He hated how the jocks bullied and made fun of him. And he hated gym class, which was just one more place to exhibit his lack of strength and coordination. To him, school was one big punishment. Oh sure, he had friends—other guys who were picked on because they weren't as big as the popular guys either. But these guys did have something going for them. They were smart and loved computers and science.

His mother tried to reassure him, saying, "Just wait, Josh. When you're fourteen, girls want the football player, but when you're thirty, they want the guy with the brains to create things like the scoreboard." But Josh wasn't comforted.

He wanted to feel important and valued *now*. He prayed that somehow God would let him be the quarterback who made the winning touchdown, instead of the water boy—just once. But taking a long look in the mirror at his reflection, he didn't see quarterback material. He was shorter and smaller than most of the guys his age.

"Your dad was the same way," his mother often reminded him. "He didn't hit his growth spurt until after he left high school. His high school friends didn't even recognize him when we returned for his ten-year reunion." So Josh resigned himself to feeling like a lightweight for the rest of high school. His only hope was that college would be better.

As he sat down to watch reruns and enjoy an after-school snack of chocolate chip cookies and Pepsi, someone banged uncontrollably on his front door. Startled, he rushed to the door and looked through the peephole. Outside, he saw Shawna, his teenage next-door neighbor, crying hysterically. As Josh opened the door, she cried, "Fire!" in between gasps.

"What? Where?" Josh cried. Then looking outside he saw black smoke pouring into the sky from her house next door. Racing to the phone, he dialed 9-1-1 and gave the necessary information to the operator. Then racing back to his front door, he watched in horror as the flames flew into the sky, coming dangerously close to his own home. He looked over at Shawna as tears poured down her face. "What happened?" he asked in desperation.

"It was a candle," she sobbed. "I only left the room for a minute. I tried to put it out, but it spread so fast. My parents aren't home, and I don't know what to do."

Suddenly, flames spread to the fence between their houses. Concerned that the fence and his house would be engulfed, Josh raced to the backyard hose. Turning the water on full force, he doused the fence and soaked the wood, the side of his house, and any nearby trees.

He heard Shawna's dog, Buster, barking in her backyard. He knew that Buster's chain was attached to the patio, so Josh handed the hose to Shawna, shimmied over the fence, and raced to free it. As he fought to loose Buster's chain, he heard the fire truck approaching. He returned to the front of his house with Buster in tow.

Josh watched as the firemen raced to put the fire out. Shortly thereafter, his mother and father arrived home, hugging him tightly. "Are you okay?" his mother asked with concern as she examined his dirty, wet clothes.

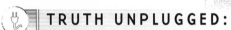

TRUTH UNPLUGGED:

Inner strength—strength of character, conviction, and courage—is more valuable than any physical strength you could ever possess.

"Yeah, Mom," Josh said and then explained to both his parents what had happened.

Awhile later, after the fire was completely extinguished, one of the firemen came over to talk to Josh and his parents. "You really did good work here," he said, looking at Josh.

"Huh? All I did was turn on the hose," Josh said.

"Actually, you did a whole lot more than that. You kept a cool head throughout the whole ordeal. If you hadn't called 9-1-1 when you did, we wouldn't have been able to save any of the house. And because you thought to hose down the fence, you saved your own house and the other houses from damage," he said pointing to the two-story home behind Shawna's. Smiling, he added, "And on top of that, you saved the dog. You can't ask for more than that. We need more young men like you." He slapped Josh on the back before walking away.

The next morning, Josh's mom called him into the kitchen and pointed to the newspaper. There, in black and white, Josh read about the fire. About midway through the article, he found a paragraph about him. The reporter referred to him as "a young hero who helped save several homes from damage due to his courage and quick thinking." Josh read the paragraph several times, trying to convince himself that it was actually talking about him. He'd never been the hero before. It was nice to know he had it in him.

Hmm—Thanks, God. Maybe for once, I did make the touchdown.

TRUTH LINK:

Dear Lord, so many times I focus on outward appearances and physical strength, but I know it's more important to have inner strength. Please help me to remember that real strength comes from You, and remind me to focus on developing my inner strength, instead of just my physique. Amen.

POWER UP:

Today's society places a lot of value on physical strength. Sports heroes are revered, and movie action heroes are admired. And although there's nothing wrong with physical strength—God definitely wants you to be healthy and fit—He's more concerned with your inner strength, the kind of strength that helps you make the right decision when difficulty comes.

Don't think you're weak just because you can't bench press a certain weight or fit into the in crowd's mold. God has given you the ability to become a very strong person as you pray, read the Bible, develop Christian friendships, and become a Godly example of how others should live. As you build your inner strength, you'll become someone others admire and want to be like.

BLACK AND WHITE

Honor

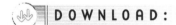

DOWNLOAD:

If your life honors the name of Jesus, he will honor you.

2 Thessalonians 1:12

"Can I take your order?" Matt asked the table of four. As the warm afternoon breeze blew onto the patio, he took his customers' orders and then went to the kitchen to turn them in to the chef. He liked working as a waiter at El Corazon Mexican Restaurant. It was his first job, and he had learned a lot in his three months there. He started as a busboy and a dishwasher, then he seated people as a host, and now, finally, he had been promoted to a waiter.

On a good night waiting tables, his tips amounted to two to three times as much as he had made busing tables. Thankfully he was able to move into the position quickly. Partly, it was due to his parents teaching him about good work habits—be on time, follow directions without complaining, be nice to everyone, and go the extra mile when asked to do something. He was surprised at how many other staff members didn't follow those same principles. They were what had helped him become a waiter faster than some of the other workers.

Matt had another reason for working so hard at this job. His father had recently been laid off from his place of employment. Though his parents hadn't asked him to help out, he felt that it was necessary to pay his own way instead of asking them for spending money. He also tried to help out with groceries and gas money for the family when he could. Every few days, he stopped at the grocery store to pick up some things he thought they needed. Sometimes he used his employee discount to bring dinner home from the restaurant. These gestures were just his way of trying to help until his father found another job.

"Hey, Matt, order for table number twenty-six is up," one of the food preparers called after Matt had turned in his latest order.

Quickly, he picked up the steaming plates of fajitas, double-checked to make sure they included pico de gallo and guacamole, and took them straight to the table. Then he checked on his other tables, refilling glasses, chips, and salsa before helping one of the busboys clear an empty table. It had taken a few weeks, but he had the routine down. He liked to stay busy and never tired of the hustle and bustle.

After they had cleared the table and the busboy headed to the kitchen, Matt looked down at the tip. It wasn't his; it belonged to Jim, one of the other waiters. He reached down and placed two dollars in his pocket. Though inside his heart pounded and his palms were sweating, he tried to continue to work as though nothing was amiss.

I didn't take all of it, he consoled himself. *And it's not like I'm taking it for myself. I'm taking it for my parents. If I can increase my tips tonight, then I can put money toward the car insurance.*

As he reasoned his action in his mind, he continued to work and felt a little better.

A few days later, he took a couple of bills from another table. Again, the tip wasn't his, but he justified it in his mind. Again and again, it happened. Over the next two weeks, he significantly increased the money he took home.

Finally one day, he heard Jim complain to a waitress in the kitchen, "My tips have really fallen lately. Some shifts I'm down about ten dollars. It's weird; I don't feel like I'm any less busy," he said. The waitress agreed that she'd noticed a fall in her earnings too. Jim continued, "If something doesn't change, I'm going to have to find another job. I can't afford to be down ten dollars each shift. It adds up. If this keeps up, I won't be able to afford my apartment this month."

 TRUTH UNPLUGGED:

Living an honorable life means living in God's truth. His truth is black and white; God doesn't live in the gray.

Matt stopped.

He hadn't considered that the other waiters needed the money just as badly as he did. *It'll be my fault if Jim can't make his rent,* Matt realized. He felt so ashamed. He saw how his actions had affected other people, and he finally admitted the truth to himself—he was stealing. *Stealing!* The thought made him sick to his stomach. *What have I been thinking? I'm a thief!*

For the rest of the night, Matt moved mechanically through his routine. He knew he wasn't giving the greatest service, but his mind was on other things. He didn't know what to do. On one hand, he could say nothing and quit taking the tips, but would that be enough? It wouldn't help Jim pay his rent or make up for the money Matt had stolen. On the other hand, if he confessed, he would lose his job. He went back and forth in his mind.

Oh Jesus, please help me get out of this, he prayed.

Unable to decide what to do, Matt continued to work for the next few days. He came in, worked his shift, and went home, taking only his tips in the process. As much as he tried to move on, he realized he couldn't just act like nothing had happened. Finally, he knew what he had to do.

Mondays were slow, but Matt knew José, the manager, came in to work on weekly reports. That afternoon, Matt nervously walked into José's office and sat down. "José, I have to resign today," he began. Confused, José asked Matt why. "I've made some mistakes that I'm not proud of." Matt gulped, feeling the truth was even uglier when spoken aloud. "I took some tip money that wasn't mine. I'm not making excuses; it was wrong. My family has had some trouble, and I just screwed up. I know I can't make up for it, but I'd appreciate it if you'd give this money to the other waiters and waitresses." From his jacket pocket, he pulled several envelopes and placed them on José's desk. Each had the name of one of the other servers on it. "I want to give them their money back."

José sat quietly in his chair, watching Matt. Finally, after several seconds of silence, he said, "Well, you're right, Matt. You can't continue to work here. It's restaurant policy—stealing is grounds for dismissal. I know it took guts to come in here like this. I appreciate your honesty, especially since you came in on your own. A lot of people would have just ignored it, even when they realized they were wrong. Because of that, and because I believe that you won't do this again, I'll give you a good reference for your next job. I won't lie, but I'll recommend that they hire you. Fair enough?" Then reaching over to pick up the envelopes, he promised to give them to the appropriate people.

Matt left José's office feeling sick that he had stolen, but lighter because he'd done the right thing and the experience was now behind him. As he walked to his car, he promised, *God, I will never do anything like this again.*

 TRUTH LINK:

Dear Lord, please forgive me for the dishonorable choices I have made. I want to live according to Your Word. Please show me how to make honorable decisions in my life, and convict me when I make the wrong ones. Amen.

POWER UP:

Have you ever made a quick decision that you later regretted? Or have you done something that goes against your morals? Maybe you tried to justify it because of extenuating circumstances, but inside you knew the truth. The good news is that God hasn't abandoned you to stagger through life lost and without His direction. He's given you the Bible, which can help you live an honorable life. In His Word, you'll find answers— answers to help you make good choices, answers to help you know how to live. God's Word is black and white, so you don't have to stumble around in the gray.

THE PROOF OF LIFE

Prayer

DOWNLOAD:

Believing-prayer will heal you, and Jesus will put you on your feet. And if you've sinned, you'll be forgiven—healed inside and out. James 5:15

Beep. Beep. Beep.

The hospital machines around Isaac's grandfather beeped and whirred. The sounds were somewhat comforting, considering their silence would have announced the end. The buzzing also helped to fill the void when Isaac didn't know what to say. He felt helpless as he watched his grandfather drift in and out of consciousness.

"Come on, Grandpa. Sit up and talk to me," he pleaded.

"Keep talking to him," one of the nurses had encouraged when she came in to change one of his intravenous bags. "He may be able to hear you."

So Isaac began to talk. He told his grandfather about his day at school, his friends, and his girlfriend; but after a while, he didn't know what else to say other than, "Please don't leave, Grandpa."

It wasn't that Isaac didn't have other family; he did. But no one—not his parents, brother, sister, grandmother, or anyone else—knew him like his grandpa did. He was convinced that his grandpa had taught him everything worth knowing about life. He'd taught him about courage, friendship, and love. Isaac had listened to everything his grandfather had said—well, almost everything.

The only thing he couldn't quite get his head around was his grandfather's faith in God. He'd attended church with his grandparents, but to Isaac it was just pretty music and plenty of words. He understood people getting together as a community—his grandfather had taught him about that too—but to put faith in something he couldn't see every day, well that was just too hard to accept.

"Isaac, would you like to come with me to the chapel to pray for your grandfather?" his grandmother asked.

"No, Grandma," Isaac responded. "I'd like to be here when the doctor comes by."

"You know, dear, the doctors don't know everything," his grandmother responded gently.

Isaac looked at her for a second before turning back to his grandfather. "The doctor is the only one who can help him now." Inside, he felt angry. What did she mean, the doctor didn't know everything? He was the only one who could offer them any help.

Thirty minutes later, the doctor came in for his morning visit. He and Isaac exchanged greetings. After watching the doctor review his grandfather's chart, Isaac asked, "How is he?"

"A little better," the doctor said, never lifting his eyes from the chart as he wrote. "The heart monitor shows an improvement in one of the areas that had been unresponsive."

Isaac was encouraged. He had confidence that whatever the doctor prescribed would work. He felt certain that the medicines would bring his grandfather home soon.

When his grandmother returned, Isaac shared the good news. His grandmother smiled knowingly, "Yes, that's what I prayed."

Isaac didn't argue with her, but he believed that it was the doctor who had helped his grandfather, not God. In Isaac's mind, God might be up there watching the events unfold, but he didn't think God really cared. God was just a silent bystander.

Another day passed, and again his grandmother invited him to go pray in the chapel. Again, Isaac declined. He waited for the doctor to make his rounds. Again, there was improvement. His grandfather had opened his eyes and had spoken to his grandmother late the previous evening. The hospital staff felt confident that he was improving.

On the following day, after another positive report, Isaac stopped the doctor on the way out of the room. "Doctor, thank you for helping my grandfather. I know if it weren't for you, my grandfather wouldn't be improving," he said.

The doctor smiled. "I wish I could take credit for his condition, but I can't. Just tell your grandmother to keep praying."

After he left, Isaac sat down beside his grandfather. He didn't know what to think. Why would his grandmother's prayers make any difference? Surely, the doctor didn't think that prayer had something to do with his grandfather's improvement. *It must just be nature taking its course,* he reasoned.

Later that evening, Isaac and his grandmother continued to sit beside his grandfather, talking to him and each other. They laughed and reminisced about a time when Isaac's grandfather had taken him across the lake by motorboat to get Saturday morning donuts.

Suddenly Isaac's grandfather opened his eyes and smiled. "I love to hear the laughter of my family," he said weakly. They rushed to his side and bent over him, laughing and encouraging him to get better. Then focusing on his wife, he said, "I've felt your prayers, Alice."

Isaac's grandmother smiled, smoothing his hair away from his face. "You didn't think I'd give you up without a fight, did you?"

He chuckled and then closed his tired eyes. "That's my girl," he said before falling asleep.

As Isaac silently watched his grandparents, a lump rose in his throat. He'd known all of his life that they followed God, but he had never been able to understand it. He'd always wanted something tangible to hold on to—something more than just a church building with people and pretty music. Now, watching them, he knew they had indeed received something tangible. Their faith was real. God had listened and answered his grandmother's prayers. His grandfather's improvement was proof of that.

TRUTH UNPLUGGED:

God wants to hear from you, so take time to talk to Him every day.

The next day, when his grandmother asked him to go to the chapel to pray, Isaac didn't hesitate. He knew he'd miss talking to the doctor, but it didn't matter. He finally understood that he would be talking to a higher source, God—Someone with more answers and more power than the doctor would ever have.

TRUTH LINK:

Dear Lord, sometimes I forget to consult You about my life. Sometimes I forget to pray about the things that concern me, but I want to change that. Help me to remember to pray and to include You in every area of my life. Amen.

POWER UP:

Prayer is an important part of living your life for God. Sometimes you'll see immediate answers to your prayers, and other times, it will take time. Regardless, continue to pray for God's presence in every situation and listen as He directs you. Look for His hand as He works things out.

You may even want to keep a notebook of the things you pray. Then, as each prayer is answered, record it. Over time, you'll see how much God has worked on your behalf. He isn't some faraway being who watches your life with mild interest. He wants to be a part of everything you do. And as you pray, He will work on your behalf.

THE SACRIFICE

Giving

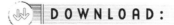 **DOWNLOAD:**

"Give away your life; you'll find life given back, but not merely given back—given back with bonus and blessing. Giving, not getting, is the way. Generosity begets generosity."

Luke 6:38

"Marty, we need to have a family meeting to talk," his father said seriously. "Go get your brother, and meet the rest of us in the living room."

Family meetings were serious. They were the kind of meetings his dad had called when his parents had decided to move the family across the country, when his mother had decided to return to work, and when his grandmother had died. Usually, they were times when the entire family would come together as a united front regarding a serious matter. Anything that needed to be said was said to everyone at the same time so that no one was left out. The meetings were usually life-changing and always put Marty on edge.

As the family came together—Marty; his mom; his dad; his brother, Ben, who was younger than he; and his sister, Meagan, who was older than he—Marty looked around for Meagan's husband, Chad. Meagan and Chad had been married a little over two years. They lived across town, close to the university, where Chad was training to be a doctor and Meagan was studying to be a teacher. Just when Marty was about to ask where Chad was, he took a closer look at Meagan. Her eyes were swollen and red from crying. *Oh man, this has to be serious,* Marty thought, hoping that something terrible hadn't happened to Chad.

"We're here together to discuss a pretty serious matter," his father began. Then looking at Meagan he asked, "Do you want to tell them?"

Meagan, who held tightly onto her mother's hand, choked out, "Chad and I are getting a divorce."

Stunned, Marty looked from his dad to his mother and then back at Meagan. He was speechless.

Meagan continued, "Chad and I have been having problems for a while now. Things have been really tight with money and school. On Monday, he told me he'd been seeing someone else and wants a divorce. Yesterday, he moved out."

Marty watched as his parents consoled and hugged Meagan.

"What this means," his father began in a shaky, emotional voice, "is that Meagan is going to move back home for a while. She can't afford her apartment all by herself. And a lawyer is going to be expensive, so we need to help her out. Marty, you're going to move in with Ben, so Meagan can have her old room back. We're all going to help her move this weekend, so any plans need to be canceled. Everyone needs to pitch in. Any questions?"

Marty couldn't think of any at the moment. He moved over to give his sister a hug, because it was the right thing to do. His mind was blank. After consoling his family for a while, he went up to his room for a retreat. He needed to collect his thoughts.

With one announcement, he'd lost a brother-in-law, gained an at-home sister, and lost his weekend and his room.

Slowly, the realization sunk in. He did feel compassionate toward his sister, but he'd waited for years to have his own room. He finally had space for all his stuff—posters, a desk, his computer, a CD player, and more. In his room, no one told him to change the music. No one got into his stuff, and he didn't have to share space with a twelve-year-old Nickelodeon junkie. Feeling slightly overwhelmed, he turned on his music and his computer. For the next two hours, he lost himself in the latest seek-and-destroy PC game.

On Saturday, Marty's parents woke everyone up early to get a head start on the day. For two days, Marty had slowly been moving his things into Ben's room. Ben

TRUTH UNPLUGGED:

As you give to others, you become God's hands to the world.

wasn't thrilled about sharing the space either, but he was quick to adjust. Since space was limited, about half of Marty's things had to go into storage. The important things, like his clothes, computer, and CD collection, moved in with him, but other things moved into the attic.

"Can't we convert the attic or basement into another bedroom for Meagan?" Marty had pleaded as he packed his things. He'd wracked his brain trying to think of an alternative to losing his room, but his parents hadn't budged. Neither the attic nor the basement was set up to be a bedroom, and converting either was too expensive to consider right now.

The family piled into a car and a truck to go to Meagan's apartment. In the truck with his dad, on the way over to Meagan's, Marty casually asked how long Meagan would be living with them.

"I'm not sure," his dad responded sadly. "I sure never saw this coming. It'll take awhile for Meagan to get on her feet again. She may not be able to move out until after she gets her degree next year."

"So I have to live with Ben for a year?" Marty asked in shock.

"Marty, trust me; this isn't easy for anyone. I know you're disappointed, but I really need you to give a little on this," his dad said, glancing over at him. "Your sister really needs our support right now." Marty didn't answer. Bummed out, he stared out the window.

Meagan's apartment was starting to look bare by the time Marty and his father arrived. Half the furniture was already gone, walls were bare, and cabinets were empty. Marty felt the hopelessness in the place. Not long before, it had been a colorful newlywed apartment with lots of life and love, but now, he felt the desperation. He walked through the small apartment labeling boxes and moving them to the door, so Ben could load the smaller ones onto the truck. In the bedroom, his sister sat on the stripped mattresses with her head in her hands, crying. Marty almost turned to leave, but then moved forward and sat beside her. He didn't know what to say, so he remained silent.

"Do you think God will forgive me?" Meagan whispered.

"For what?" Marty asked earnestly. "God knows Chad left, not you." His protective, brotherly nature rose to attention.

Meagan let out a cynical chuckle. "Yeah, he left alright. I feel like such a failure. Here I am, a twenty-one-year-old soon-to-be divorcée who lives at home with her parents and steals her kid brother's room. Something is definitely wrong with this picture."

One glance at his distraught sister, and Marty knew sharing his room was a minor thing. Putting his arm around her, he gave her a quick hug. Feeling his emotions rising in his throat, he tried to lighten the mood. "Well, you can have the room, but the bathroom is another thing. I'm not waiting for two hours each morning for you to get ready. There's a garden hose in the backyard. That's it. That's all you get," he teased. Hearing her laugh, he knew he'd accomplished his goal.

Within a few hours, Meagan's apartment was empty, and the family turned to leave. Watching his sister take one last, sad look around the apartment, Marty knew, at that moment, he'd give her anything. He wasn't looking forward to bunking with Ben, but he realized his room would be more than just a room for Meagan. It would be a refuge, the home that she needed right now, and that was one thing Marty could do to help her during this difficult chapter in her life.

 TRUTH LINK:

Dear Lord, please help me to have a giving heart. I want to remember that some things are bigger than I am and that I don't always have to have my way. But sometimes I forget. Sometimes I can't see past my own wants and needs. Please remind me to put others first. Amen.

 POWER UP:

A giving heart is more than just giving your tithes or your offerings. Although those are very important, sometimes it is harder to give of yourself. It's hard to defer to others' needs and put them first, but that's exactly what God asks us to do. As Christians, He wants us to be participants in caring for each other. You're important, and what you give to others is important. So the next time you're asked or feel led to give of yourself for someone else, remember that God is working through you. You are His hands and feet to others, and that's a very important part to play.

NO ONE WILL EVER KNOW

Sex

DOWNLOAD:

There's more to sex than mere skin on skin. Sex is as much spiritual mystery as physical fact. As written in Scripture, "The two become one." Since we want to become spiritually one with the Master, we must not pursue the kind of sex that avoids commitment and intimacy, leaving us more lonely than ever—the kind of sex that can never "become one." 1 Corinthians 6:16-17

"Quint, you look great," Jennifer said as he climbed in the car. "I love that jacket."

"Thanks. I thought it might get cold tonight at the fair" he responded.

As Mitch drove the three of them toward the fairgrounds, they discussed their favorite rides. Mitch voted for the Tilt-A-Whirl. "I like to spin so fast the whole world's a blur."

"I love the Ferris wheel!" Jennifer exclaimed. "I love to get up high and see all over."

"No way!" Mitch laughed. "I get woozy when I get that high."

"Well, Quint will just have to take me," Jennifer said smoothly, sending Quint a glimmering smile.

He laughed. "Sure. I don't mind."

Quint had been concerned about tagging along on Mitch and Jennifer's date, but they had insisted. "Other people will be there. By the end of the night, there will probably be a bunch of us hanging out together. Besides, Jennifer wants you to go," Mitch had said.

Mitch and Jennifer had been together for a few months, and Quint was happy for his best friend. Jennifer was beautiful and spunky. She'd pursued Mitch for a while before he'd finally asked her out. Her persistence was one of the things Mitch admired most. "She doesn't play games. She goes after what she wants."

At the fair, they bought their tickets, played games, and rode rides. Then, Jennifer hooked her arm around Quint's. "The Ferris wheel is calling my name. Mitch, why don't you wait for us over at the concession stand? We'll be back." Before long, they climbed into the seat and inched their way to the top, as other seats unloaded and reloaded.

"Quint, you're a really good friend to Mitch. He talks about you all the time. It's always 'Quint this' and 'Quint that,'" Jennifer laughed, tossing her hair back. "Sometimes I think I chose the wrong boyfriend."

Quint chuckled, "Well, we've known each other forever. He's a good guy."

"Yeah, I know. I just think you're more sensitive," she responded, wrapping her arm around his.

Is she just being nice, or is she actually flirting with me? Quint wondered.

Then, she laid her head on his shoulder. Trying to resist her strawberry-scented hair, he pointed to some spot in the distance with the arm she held. She was his best friend's girlfriend, and he respected that. Although he wasn't entirely sure what was happening, he knew they were dangerously close to crossing a line.

"You know, no one would have to know if you kissed me," she whispered in his ear.

"You're *Mitch's* girlfriend, Jennifer." Quint felt trapped. Unfortunately, he was trapped with a really pretty girl.

"If you don't tell, I won't either," she said as she snuggled closer, laying a hand on his chest as she kissed his neck.

Though the evening was cool, Quint felt like he'd landed in the middle of an inferno. The Ferris wheel began to move around and around. "I—have to pass," Quint stammered.

Jennifer pulled away and smiled. "A challenge. I like that." Then laying a hand on his thigh, she leaned in again. "Trust me, you'd enjoy it. All of it."

Quint quickly grabbed her hand, thankful that the ride had come to an end. As they exited the Ferris wheel, Mitch joined them. "How was it?"

Jennifer smiled. "Great, but I think Quint needs a drink. He got a little jumpy up there."

"Too much for ya, huh?" Mitch chuckled, slugging Quint in the arm.

Quint smiled half-heartedly. *You have no idea.*

Later at home, Quint lay on his bed staring at the ceiling. He tried to understand why Jennifer had made a pass at him. Was she unhappy with Mitch? Did she really like him better? Regardless, Quint couldn't imagine ever dating her. Not only was she Mitch's girlfriend, but she was way too fast for him.

The next week in school, as Quint came out of his biology class, he saw Jennifer waiting for him. "Hey, Quint. I've missed seeing you lately," she said innocently.

"I've been busy." Quint began walking to his next class, wishing she hadn't met him like this. If Mitch saw them together, he might suspect something. So what if she was pretty and fun. She was Mitch's girlfriend. Quint kept reminding himself of that fact.

"Hey, I'm having a few friends over this Friday. Mitch has to work, but I hope you'll come. It starts at eight," she said. Then, nudging him, she added, "Don't worry. I'll behave myself."

After talking to Mitch, Quint decided it was safe to go. Jennifer had invited about six other friends. They would watch movies and order pizza. When Quint arrived, he didn't see any other cars or hear anyone inside. He rang the doorbell. Jennifer slowly opened the door. She wore a short, floral dress with spaghetti straps. When she led Quint into the living room, he noticed they were alone. Candles filled the room, and he heard soft music coming from somewhere.

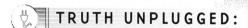

TRUTH UNPLUGGED:

God isn't punishing you by asking you to save sex for marriage. He's protecting you from making decisions that will hurt you in the long run.

"Where is everyone?" he asked. Although inside, he already suspected no one else was coming.

"I changed my mind. I thought a party of two would be more fun," Jennifer said, taking his jacket. "You want something to drink? I have regular and diet."

"Regular's fine. Where are your parents?"

"They're out for the evening. They won't be back until late," she said as she returned to the living room with his drink. "Have a seat."

Quint sat on the edge of the sofa and watched as Jennifer joined him. "So what should we do?" she asked teasingly, as she moved closer to him.

"What are you doing, Jennifer? You're Mitch's girlfriend."

She gave him a seductive smile and leaned in to kiss him. "Like I said on the Ferris wheel, no one will ever know."

Quint shot off the sofa like he'd been burned. "This is wrong." A thousand thoughts rushed through his mind. He could lose his best friend. Not to mention, he was pretty sure Jennifer had more in mind than just kissing.

"Who says so?" She rose from the sofa and walked towards him, pulling him in for a kiss. "Trust me."

As he pulled away, Quint looked her dead in the eye, "Like Mitch trusts you?"

Surprise and anger crossed her face. "Who do you think you are? Do you *know* what I'm offering you?"

"I have a pretty good idea," Quint said. "And although part of me is tempted and flattered, the other part—the bigger part—can't let anything happen. Not only is Mitch my best friend, but I don't believe in sex outside of marriage."

Angry, Jennifer sputtered insults at him. "You don't deserve to be here. Do you really think you're such a prize that I should have to beg you to be with me? You're nothing to me—just something to pass my time. Now, get out!"

Quint grabbed his jacket and left. Though he didn't want to, he headed toward Mitch's house. He knew he couldn't keep quiet about what had happened. Realizing he should have said something sooner, Quint tried to imagine how Mitch would respond— anger, blame, hurt. Regardless, Quint had to come clean. He knew Jennifer's anger wouldn't disappear over the weekend, and Mitch would eventually find out. *I might as well deal with it now,* Quint thought as he tried to think of how to tell Mitch the truth.

Lord, thanks for getting me out of there. Now, help me tell Mitch, he prayed.

TRUTH LINK:

Dear Lord, please help me to be strong when it comes to sexual temptation. You know what it's like these days. I want to abstain from sex, but I need Your help. Please show me the people I should be around and whom I should date. Amen.

POWER UP:

Everywhere we look, we're surrounded by sex. TV shows joke about it. Movies show it. Advertising sells with it. It's portrayed as casual, something to be expected in any dating relationship that lasts longer than a month. But the truth is, sex is special and spiritual. God wants you to enjoy it within the boundaries of marriage.

He isn't **PUNISHING** you by dictating that sex should be saved for marriage. Instead, He's **PROTECTING** you from a lot of hurt. By saving sex, you won't be at high risk for unwanted pregnancies, diseases, and endless broken hearts. You won't be filled with regrets about relationships that went too far too quickly.

Instead, you'll know the spiritual and physical fulfillment that comes from experiencing sex with your spouse. Regardless of whether you're a virgin or not, make the decision today to save sex for marriage. You'll be glad you did.

THE REALITY OF IT ALL

Fantasy

DOWNLOAD:

Against all illusion and fantasy and empty talk there's always this rock foundation: Fear God! Ecclesiastes 5:7

"Have you seen the new Avenging Riders game?" Alonzo asked as he took a bite of his Salisbury steak. "It is so cool. I've been playing it over the Internet with people from all over the world. I'm Goth, the Bounty Hunter. Last night I rode into an alien city and freed five of my brothers-in-arms. It was so cool!"

"I've read several reviews on it," Thomas said. "It looks incredible. They say the graphics are way better than anything else on the market."

"Yeah, they're totally awesome—so much better than Quantum Nemesis," Alonzo said. "Why don't you come over after school and check it out?"

"That'd be great. I'll see you in English," Thomas said as he left the lunch table for his next class.

After school, Thomas went to Alonzo's house. Looking at the screen, he couldn't remember ever seeing a game that looked so realistic. "I have *got* to get this game," he exclaimed.

On Saturday, Thomas bought his copy from the local software store, installed it, and devoured the instruction guide. He set up his player profile and began to play. His character, a rogue arms dealer named Quiznar, was burly and commanding. Thomas had intentionally chosen him for his size and strength. Other characters respected him at first glance.

For the next day and a half, Thomas continued to play. He familiarized himself with the computerized land. He met other players, formed strategic bonds, and learned how to wield the weapons.

Thomas felt invincible.

On Monday, he joined Alonzo at lunch. "Man, I *love* that game! I'm hooked big time." Alonzo agreed, the game was great. They spent their entire lunch period talking about their weekend gaming, discussing strategy and protocol.

For the next couple of weeks, whenever Thomas wasn't at school, he played Avenging Riders. He progressed further and further in the game, became stronger, and earned more points. At night, he played as long as he could. He lived for the weekends when he could play all day Saturday and before and after church on Sunday.

One Monday, during lunch, Alonzo asked, "How did you make out on your English project?"

Thomas looked blankly at him.

"Remember, the project where we had to interview people about the importance of communication in the workplace?"

Thomas shook his head and shrugged. "I forgot all about it."

"How could you forget about something that's worth 30 percent of your grade?" Alonzo stared at him in shock. "If you don't turn it in, the highest you can make in the class is a D."

Again Thomas shrugged indifferently and returned to eating his turkey tetrazini. He'd totally forgotten about the assignment. In fact, he hadn't thought of school all weekend. He'd played Avenging Riders. As he thought about the game, he wondered what it would be like if he were really Quiznar, a rogue arms dealer. He wouldn't have to think about English projects, school lunches, tests, or nosey friends. He could just march out the door, eliminating anyone in his way. He looked around the cafeteria and planned how Quiznar would escape this stronghold. He would, of course, have several weapons hidden on him, but no one would stop him anyway. They'd be too afraid of his strength. He was a dangerous person who didn't answer to anyone.

After school, Thomas took refuge in his room, playing Avenging Riders. He hadn't turned his computer off since he started the game. He would play before school and after school. And even during school he would make plans of what he'd do and where he'd go.

The following day, Alonzo asked, "Thomas, do you want to come over and have a sci-fi fest this weekend? I just got *Attack of the Clones* on DVD. It should be fun watching the extra footage."

Thomas thought about it but couldn't imagine leaving his computer. He'd made it to a new area and had almost become a master player. He couldn't give that up. "Thanks, but I can't. I have something else to do this weekend."

"Like what?" Alonzo asked.

"I just made it to the Trafalgar Gate. I can't stop just yet. I'm almost a master. If I can just figure out how to . . . " He stopped as he saw Alonzo's reaction.

Alonzo frowned. "Man, you know it's just a game, right? You're not really a rogue arms dealer. You're just a guy who's playing a computer game. How many hours do you spend on that thing anyway?"

"I don't know. Maybe seven."

"Seven hours a week?"

"No, seven a day. And it's not *just* a game," Thomas exploded. "I've put a lot of time in on it. And I'm not going to miss the chance to become a master. You just don't understand. It's important."

Alonzo looked at him in shock. "You are way too into this. You are spending seven hours a day on it; that's close to fifty hours a week. Man, you're obsessed!"

"That's crazy!" Thomas stormed away. *If this was the Avenging Riders' universe, Alonzo would be history,* he thought. Shocked at his own thoughts, he stopped and turned to watch Alonzo walk away. Did he really wish that he could kill his best friend? Where had that thought come from?

TRUTH UNPLUGGED:

Your mind is a precious gift from God that must be exercised and controlled. Don't let destructive thoughts consume you. Instead think on good things that produce life in you.

Throughout the rest of the day, he thought about what Alonzo had said. Was it true? Was he really obsessed with Avenging Riders? He'd heard about people becoming addicted to video games, but surely he didn't fall into that category. Then again, he honestly didn't like to think of it as a game. He liked being Quiznar. He liked being strong and powerful and having people be afraid of him. He liked controlling whether others lived or died. He liked the respect that came with having the title of a master player.

It was a far cry from his real life where he felt like an outsider so much of the time. Sure, people thought he was smart, but most didn't necessarily want to hang out with him. He wasn't strong and powerful. He was average—average height, average weight, average looks, and average athletic ability. Nothing about him stood out.

After school that day, he played the game with less enthusiasm. He saw other players dodging, running, and fighting, but he felt empty. Over the last few weeks, his entire life had revolved around his computer, and what did he have to show for it? His grades had slipped. He'd mentally checked out of everything else in his life, even if he still went through the motions. And now he was fighting with his best friend. For the first time, he questioned whether the game was really worth it. If he continued down this road, his life would become more limited. But could he just walk away now? He wrestled with the question of what to do.

Without thinking, his hand shot out and hit the power switch to his computer. In a flash, the screen went black. His heart raced. In one second, his emotions ranged from joy to fear, happiness to agony. He'd turned the game off. He backed away from his computer as though it were reaching out for him. When had he let this thing become so big? When had he let it become a part of him? When had it gotten such a strong hold on him?

Crawling onto his bed, he picked up his phone and dialed Alonzo's number. "I turned it off," Thomas said quietly without introducing himself. He continued watching the computer.

"Hey man, I'm glad. I was starting to worry about you," Alonzo said. "Do you want me to come over?"

"I don't know. I feel really weird, like I don't know what to do with myself."

"I think it's called withdrawal. I'll be right over," Alonzo said.

As he hung up the phone, Thomas looked around his room. He felt like he was coming out of a fog. It was the first time in weeks that he'd seen—really seen—anything. He noticed that the floor was covered with dirty clothes and trash. His room needed to be cleaned. *It's a place to start,* he thought as he began moving around the room. As he cleared the floor and put things away, his mind began to clear too.

TRUTH LINK:

Dear Lord, thank You for giving me a clear mind and for helping me keep my imagination in check. Help me avoid destructive thoughts and anything that would try to control my thoughts. Help me fill my mind with the good things in Your Word. Amen.

 POWER UP:

God has given you a powerful tool—your mind. He's given you your imagination and the ability to dream, but be careful not to allow your thoughts to become obsessive or destructive. Don't allow yourself to become a slave to your imagination by entertaining thoughts of hatred, violence, or lust. If you entertain those thoughts, they will begin to alter how you view your life and others around you. Destructive thoughts will begin to affect how you live.

God has so much more for you. He wants you to use your mind for His plans, for your own good, and for the good of others, not for darkness. When negative thoughts come to you, take a moment to ask God to help you control them. Reading your Bible will help you think like God thinks and to think on His plans. It may take time, but God will help you train your mind to think on good things.

TURN ON THE LIGHT

Encouragement

Lamont took his seat next to the window in the coach portion of the airplane. He stuffed his backpack under the seat in front of him and excitedly watched the airline workers load the suitcases and direct the other planes. He was on his way to visit his grandparents at their ranch, and he couldn't wait to get there.

Each summer, his dad sent him to visit them, so he could ride horses and "stay in touch with his roots," as his dad put it. As an architect, his dad had to live in the city, but Lamont knew his father missed the country. He knew it was important to him that Lamont love it too, and he did. He dreamed of becoming a veterinarian with a farm and animals some day.

Next to him, a woman sat down. She moved quickly and decisively. Everything about her—her tailored suit, coiffed hair, pearl jewelry, and Louis Vitton handbag—screamed Serious Business Woman. *She's probably a corporate lawyer,* Lamont thought as he looked down at his own jeans and sweatshirt. The woman adjusted her seat, pulled a large file folder out of her briefcase, and shoved the rest of her things under the seat in front of her. Then she began to read her documents, oblivious to everyone around her.

Definitely, a lawyer, Lamont thought as he glanced at the formal-looking documents the woman read.

Turning his attention back to the workers outside the plane, he felt the excitement he always experienced when he flew. He loved it. He knew that many people hated to fly, but he loved the thought of soaring through the air, crossing the country in a matter of hours, and seeing people from all over the world.

Glancing around at the other passengers, all different ages and races, he wondered where they were going, where they were from, why they were traveling. Were they, like him, going to visit family, or were they on business? Lamont loved to imagine their stories. Looking over at the grandmotherly type sitting in the seat across the aisle, he imagined she was on her way to visit her new grandbaby. And the techie-looking guy next to him was probably on his way to a Star Trek convention. *Oh yeah,* he thought, smiling to himself, *definitely a Trekie.*

After takeoff, Lamont retrieved his CD player from his backpack and settled back for a quiet ride. Awhile later, the flight attendants came around with drinks and a snack. Lamont removed his earphones and opened his package of pretzels. Then, the woman next to him introduced herself as Maggie.

"What music are you listening to?" she asked.

Swallowing a mouthful of pretzels, he choked out, "Beveled."

"I'm not familiar with them," she responded as she opened her snack.

"They're a new Christian band."

Maggie slid a surprised glance toward Lamont. "You're a Christian then, huh?" When Lamont said yes, the woman made a quick face. "I'm not religious myself. I can't convince myself that there's a god up there who knows my name. It all seems like fantasy."

Lamont smiled but didn't respond immediately. He thought back to a time when he would've agreed. He'd been in church on Christmas and Easter, but it was all a bunch of repetitious fables to him. Then he saw the truth. "Once I would have agreed with you," he said simply, "but then I realized there is a God who cares. It changed my life."

Maggie gave him an appeasing smile. "And what changed your mind?" she asked as though waiting for Lamont to reveal some trivial approach to life.

"My mom died," Lamont said quietly. "No one could comfort me—not my family, not counselors or friends. No one. Then one day I prayed, and I felt an overwhelming sense of comfort. And there was something I had heard at church one Easter that I couldn't get out of my mind. So I went back. It was like Someone turned the light on inside me."

Maggie stopped eating while Lamont spoke and then continued eating her pretzels in silence, as if she were considering what Lamont had said.

Lamont didn't see himself as an evangelist, and he didn't share his faith with every stranger he met. But if prompted, he would talk about it. Jesus had changed his life. He was convinced of it. He hadn't grown up in Sunday school, knowing all the ins and outs of Christianity. Instead, he'd come to his faith with nothing. Other than the Easter and Christmas sermons, he hadn't known anything. So when his life changed, when he finally felt alive again after his mother's death, he knew it was real. There was no other explanation.

"Do you think God hears your prayers?" she asked quietly.

Lamont noticed that Maggie no longer looked like the no-nononsense businesswoman she had earlier. Instead, she looked uncertain and even fearful. "Yes, I do. He doesn't always answer them the way I want, but I believe He hears and answers them."

Maggie sat quietly, as if she were considering Lamont's answer. "You know where I'm going?" Without giving him time to answer, she said, "To my father's funeral."

"I'm sorry," Lamont said quietly.

"It's okay, really. We didn't get along. He wasn't around much when I was growing up, but I guess—I guess I had hoped we still had time to work things out."

TRUTH UNPLUGGED:

Your words can bring healing to others in difficult situations.

Lamont didn't know what to say. He knew this woman was hurting. "Maybe you should try praying about it."

The woman turned to him and then with a shake of her head dismissed it. "He wouldn't hear me anyway."

"You might be surprised. Like I told you, it changed my life. If you want, I'll pray with you," Lamont offered. Lamont watched as tears came to the woman's eyes, and she said okay.

Lamont bowed his head and closed his eyes. He prayed that the woman would have peace and comfort through her difficult time. He prayed that God would help her have closure with her father in her heart, and then he prayed that she would realize that Jesus loved her.

When they finished praying, Maggie wiped the tears from her eyes. For the rest of their flight, they talked about their lives. Lamont told her about his summer vacation and his grandparents' ranch. Maggie told him about her high-rise apartment and career. After the flight, Lamont and Maggie said good-bye. Lamont promised to continue to pray for her.

As he joined his grandparents, he felt like he'd just made a friend. Although they probably wouldn't see each other again, Lamont knew they had shared an important moment. He'd been there when Maggie needed a friend. Realizing that God had put them next to each other on that flight was just one more reason Lamont believed.

TRUTH LINK:

Dear Lord, help me to see opportunities in which I can encourage others. I want to be sensitive to others when they need to hear that You love them. Then when the time comes, I'll share Your words of hope. Amen.

POWER UP:

Have you ever found yourself in a situation where you wanted to encourage or help someone through a difficult time, but you weren't sure what to say? It happens to everyone. Sometimes the person in trouble needs you to listen, offer support, or do something. In those moments, don't underestimate prayer. Sometimes, your sympathy and advice aren't the best remedy. Even if you don't pray out loud, you can still pray silently that God will give you the words to say. As you do this, you will become a tool He can use to help a person who is hurting.

THE GRACE TO LIVE AT HOME

Difficult Parents

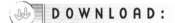 **DOWNLOAD:**

You have turned for me my mourning into dancing; You have put off my sackcloth and clothed me with gladness.

Psalm 30:11 NKJV

"Leo, where are you?" his father bellowed as he walked in the door. "Why isn't dinner ready? You know, you're worthless. I work all day, and all I ask is that you keep the house from looking like a pigsty and heat up a TV dinner every once in a while. You're just plain worthless." He threw his jacket across the dining room table, covering the dishes that were set for dinner.

Hearing him, Leo stopped doing his homework and returned to the kitchen to finish dinner. "It's ready. I was just waiting for you," he countered snippily. He knew it didn't do any good, but sometimes he couldn't help fighting back just a little.

"You gettin' smart with me? I put a roof over your head and make sure you have food to eat, and you want to smart off to me?" He eyed Leo, ready for a fight.

Leo could tell his father was in one of his moods, and it probably wouldn't improve. The best he could do was stay out of his way. Without saying a word, he fixed their plates. Then sitting down at the table, they began to eat. After a few bites, his father shoved the plate away. "Can't you make a simple meal without it tasting like garbage?" Taking the plate to the sink, he threw the dinner down the disposal and tossed the plate onto the counter with a clatter. "I'm going out. Have this place cleaned up by the time I get back."

Numbly, Leo finished his meal and cleaned the kitchen. He knew the signs. By the time his father returned, he needed to be out of sight. Two years ago, his mother had left them. Leo still didn't know why his mother hadn't taken him too. That fact still stung.

His father had always been difficult. He was angry most of the time, yelling at, or even hitting, whoever was closest. That's what tonight was—a get-drunk-and-hit-something night. Leo actually preferred that his father leave, although he'd probably end up at the corner bar. Maybe he'd take his anger out on someone down there or be so tired when he came home that he'd go straight to bed.

Most of the time, Leo could handle him. And when things got too bad, he slept either at a friend's or outside, anywhere his father couldn't find him. Usually, by the morning, his dad had either forgotten or dismissed anything he'd done the night before.

As the evening passed, Leo finished his homework and prepared for the next day. Since he worked after school, he had to prepare everything, so he could move from one thing to the next quickly. He also took time to clean the bathroom and vacuum. Looking around the living room, he decided to dust and

Windex later. All in all, the house looked pretty good. At least his father wouldn't explode over it.

The next morning before school, his friend Alan met him at his locker, "Hey, a few of us are going to a concert next weekend. There'll be a few bands there—Charged and Effervescence. You've heard me play their CDs. You wanna go?"

Leo considered it. "How much would it cost?" he asked. He had to be tight with his money. Though he made money at his after-school job, most of it went into savings for college. He only had about forty dollars in spending money, and he sure couldn't waste it.

"Only twenty-five dollars," Alan answered. "Come on; it'll be fun."

Alan constantly invited Leo to Christian events. Most of Alan's friends were Christians, and Leo always had fun when he joined them. Most everyone was really nice and made him feel welcome. "I'll think about it," he said.

After school Leo went to work, cooking and waiting tables at a downtown diner. He worked there from 3 P.M. to 6 P.M. each weekday and then all day every other Saturday. Although the pay wasn't great, he made a good amount in tips from the professional types.

Later at home, he set the table and unwrapped the container of meatloaf and mashed potatoes that he'd brought home from the diner. His father arrived home around seven, which he usually did each night. They sat together at the dinner table, although Leo didn't know why, since they rarely spoke. He just knew that if he didn't have the table set and dinner ready, his father got angry. He constantly reminded Leo that "it was the least he could do."

"Dad, my friend Alan asked me to go to a concert this Saturday," he began carefully. It's a Christian concert, so it won't be wild or anything. I wouldn't be here for dinner, but I'd make sure you had something to eat."

His father didn't respond for a few seconds. His head bowed toward his plate, he continued eating. "Waste of money," he grunted. "I ain't payin' for it."

"I have money. It's really not that much." When his father didn't respond after a few minutes, he asked, "So can I go?"

"I don't care what you do," his father responded as he rose to leave the table. "Just don't come home drunk or stoned. And if you get thrown in jail, don't call me." Then he left the kitchen.

On Saturday, Leo enjoyed the concert. Though he didn't know the songs, he still enjoyed screaming, clapping, and dancing with the rest of the crowd. At the end of the last band's set, the lead singer invited anyone who hadn't made Jesus their personal Lord and Savior to come to the front to pray with someone. He said that Jesus loved each person just the way they were, and because of that love, Jesus had died for their sins. All anyone had to do was accept His love, renounce their old ways, and live their lives for Him.

Leo didn't understand everything the singer said, but he knew he wanted to know the kind of love the guy spoke of. Suddenly, before he could think, he moved into the aisle and walked toward the front. A college-age guy name Todd met him and prayed with him. Unable to believe the peace and love that swept over him, Leo began to cry.

All the pain that he'd buried deep inside came to the surface. He felt the pain from his mother's abandonment. He felt the sting of his father's abuse. He felt the hurt of feeling so alone, unloved, and unwanted. He felt the wound of bearing so much responsibility. As all the pain came to the surface, he felt some force sweep it all away. The longer he stayed, the lighter he felt.

Afterwards, Alan slapped him on the back. "I'm so glad you went down there. I've been praying for you for a long time."

"You have?" Leo asked in amazement.

Alan nodded. "I know things aren't easy for you, Leo. You never say anything, but I can tell. It's good that you don't have to handle it all on your own anymore."

"That's really nice to know," Leo agreed.

The rest of the evening passed uneventfully, but Leo couldn't remember when he had been so happy. He talked with the others on his way home. When he walked in the door to his house, he heard his father's slow, steady breaths coming from his recliner. He'd fallen asleep in front of the TV. Watching him sleep, Leo knew that his father hadn't changed, but the dull numbness Leo had felt was gone. Now, he just felt peaceful, and that was enough for now.

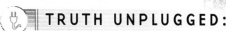 **TRUTH UNPLUGGED:**

If you have difficult parents, God can change their hearts and give you the grace to live with them.

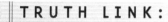

TRUTH LINK:

Dear Lord, You know what my home is like. You know when it isn't loving or peaceful. I pray that You will continue to work in my parents so that one day they will come to know You. Until then, I pray that You would give me the grace to live with them. Amen.

POWER UP:

Wouldn't it be nice if everyone had a loving family who listens, loves, and wants the best for each other? Instead, you may live in a difficult situation. Your parents may be drug addicts or alcoholics. Your home may be physically or verbally abusive. If you are in danger or it's bad enough that you need to leave, get help from a relative, school counselor, pastor, or other adult.

Remember, only God can change your parents' hearts, and even then, they must make the decision to allow God to change them. Until then, continue to pray for them. Ask God to help you live with them, and find supportive Christian friends whom you can turn to. Don't believe that your parents' actions are your fault. Don't be ashamed or feel that there must be something wrong with you. There isn't. God is working on your behalf. He created you. He loves you, and He wants to help you.

RIGHT BEFORE MY EYES

Pornography

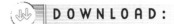

DOWNLOAD:

Your old life is dead. Your new life, which is your real life—even though invisible to spectators—is with Christ in God. He is your life . . . . And that means killing off everything connected with that way of death: sexual promiscuity, impurity, lust, doing whatever you feel like whenever you feel like it, and grabbing whatever attracts your fancy. That's a life shaped by things and feelings instead of by God. Colossians 3:3, 5

Captivated, Jamie stared at the images on his computer screen. Though he'd been warned about visiting pornographic sites, he couldn't help his curiosity. At first, he'd been shocked by what he saw, but slowly, he overcame the shock. Now, he craved it. At night, after his mother went to bed, he surfed the Internet. His fascination had started innocently enough. He'd just typed in one or two words, but before long he scanned through hundreds, maybe even thousands, of pictures of real women.

Jamie knew people warned against looking at the images, and of course, his mother wouldn't approve. But after looking at them several times, he wasn't sure what the problem was. Sure, he'd felt a little guilty, but that passed. It wasn't like he was hurting anyone.

The next day after school, he joined his two best friends, Lamar and Michelle, at Taco Bell for an after-school snack. They liked to make a Taco Bell run about once a week. It was fun to talk and joke around with these friends he'd known since preschool. After he admitted that he'd visited pornographic sites, they looked at him in shock.

"That's so disgusting!" Michelle responded. "Why would you want to look at stuff like that, Jamie?"

"What's the harm?" he answered. "They're just pictures. It's not like some real, naked woman showed up in my room."

"Not that you'd mind if she did," Lamar joked, wiggling his eyebrows up and down.

Jamie laughed as Michelle looked in horror from Lamar to Jamie, "It's not funny. It's sick!"

Over the next few weeks, Jamie continued to surf the Web sites. He even visited a few sites with downloadable videos, so he could watch films. He began daydreaming about the films and the pictures he'd seen. He began imagining different scenarios in his mind. He imagined his young gym teacher in one of the outfits or settings he'd seen. He imagined Alexa Micheals, the girls' star basketball player, doing some of the things he'd seen in the films.

"You can close your mouth now," Michelle said one day as she and Jamie were watching Alexa practice on the basketball court.

"What? I wasn't doing anything," Jamie responded, embarrassed at having been caught in his daydream.

"Yeah, you were about to start panting. What's with you anyway?" Michelle said, giving his shoulder a shove.

"Nothing," Jamie said. "I'm just watching her play."

Michelle watched him for a minute, but Jamie wouldn't look her in the eye for fear that she would see the truth.

The next week the three friends met at Taco Bell again. Jamie noticed a couple come in and place an order. Watching the woman, he stared, captivated. Some would have called her voluptuous, but he just thought she was hot. In his mind, he slowly peeled her clothes away.

"Hello," Michelle said, waving her hand in front of his eyes. "You're panting again."

"Huh?" Jamie said, shaking his head as if trying to free himself from the vision.

Lamar laughed. "Man, you were out of it," he said, looking over at the woman. "Enjoying the view?"

Jamie shrugged as Michelle shook her head. "You were undressing her in your mind, weren't you?"

TRUTH UNPLUGGED:

Pornography hurts everyone by degrading others and preventing you from having rewarding relationships.

"No!" Jamie lied. Michelle continued to watch him with a look that said she didn't believe him.

The following week after school, Jamie noticed Michelle wearing a new pink tank top. She looked pretty good. "Nice shirt," he said, letting his eyes trail her up and down.

Slowly, she responded with a frown, "Thanks."

"You should wear more shirts like that. They really show off your figure," he said, allowing his eyes to rest on her body.

Michelle snatched her backpack in front of her, hugging it fiercely. "Get away from me, Jamie," she hissed. "You make me sick!"

"What?" Jamie said in mock innocence.

Michelle's eyes hardened. "I am *not* one of your sick fantasies. Don't look at me like I'm one of the tramps on those sites you visit," she said, her voice rising in anger.

Embarrassed, Jamie looked around as other people heard her yelling at him. "Calm down, Michelle. I was just trying to pay you a compliment."

"Give me break. You look at me like I'm a piece of meat, and you expect me to be grateful. You really are sick. Get away from me!" She stormed off.

Lamar, who'd been standing a few feet away, joined Jamie. "What was that all about?"

Flustered, Jamie tried to explain. "I just told her that she looked nice, and she freaked out."

Lamar watched him for a few seconds. "If you looked at her like you've been looking at other girls lately, she probably had a reason."

"What's that supposed to mean?" Jamie asked, shocked.

"It means, get your mind out of the gutter. Look, Michelle's my friend too, and she doesn't fly off the handle at just anything. And you've been staring at girls like they're dancing around poles naked. Just get it together," Lamar said as he walked away.

Jamie walked out of school feeling confused. Had he really been so transparent that everyone could tell what he was thinking? Had he really allowed himself to view Michelle like one of the women on the sites? Thinking about it, he realized it was true. He *had* treated Michelle like a piece of meat. In fact, he'd viewed most of the women he'd seen lately like they were images on one of the pornography sites. His face burned with embarrassment and shame.

Hopeful that Michelle would forgive him, he set off to apologize to her. He didn't quite know how he'd get past this with her, but their friendship was too old to just throw away. He also needed to thank Lamar for telling him the truth. He knew it would take effort to stop looking at the pictures since they'd become such a normal part of his life and they were so accessible, but he finally realized how pornography really could harm people. If he didn't quit, he'd probably lose his best friends. There's no way it was worth that.

TRUTH LINK:

Dear Lord, help me to stay away from pornography and all ungodly images and thoughts. I want to keep Your viewpoint so I can stay away from any image or thought that's out of line with Your will—in pictures, movies, even music. Thank You for giving me a fresh perspective so I won't view others in demeaning ways. Amen.

POWER UP:

Have you ever heard people try to rationalize pornography? They call it art or freedom of expression, and they claim that there's nothing wrong with it. The problem is, those images degrade others and that **is** wrong.

If you allow yourself to view and dwell on those images, lust will begin to consume you. You will no longer be able to see people with respect and appreciation; instead, you will begin to measure them by the images you've seen. In the end, pornography hurts you too. It stops you from having rewarding and healthy relationships because you can't get past the images in your mind.

The best way to avoid these consequences is to refuse to look at pornography in the first place. However, if you have already crossed that line, stop right now and ask God to forgive you and to cleanse you. Then, refuse to look at pornographic images again. God will give you the grace to do it.

MAKING THE TIME COUNT

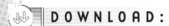

Attitude

⬇ DOWNLOAD:

A cheerful disposition is good for your health; gloom and doom leave you bone-tired. Proverbs 17: 22

"Hi, welcome to the Sub Shack. What can I get you tonight?" Wes asked through the microphone.

"I'll have a large roast beef sub with everything on it, a bag of chips, and a medium Coke," the faceless customer ordered.

Wes gave the customer the total and then made his way to the preparation bar to make the sub sandwich. Oh, how he hated this job. He needed to work, and the Sub Shack was one of the only fast-food joints that closed on Sundays so he could still go to church with his family. At first, he thought it would be cool since he liked the sandwiches. But now, just the sight of a huge slab of processed lunch meat made him sick, not to mention the smells—onions, pickles, jalapeño peppers. And then there was the sticky film that covered the floors and counters from the soda fountain. He hated that too.

Wes had decided to get a job because he needed gas money for his car and so he could go out with his friends. Now, most of his nights were either spent working or catching up on homework from the nights when he had to work. It was a vicious circle.

Why couldn't I have just been born rich? he wondered constantly.

"Wes, do you have that roast beef sub ready yet?" his manager Chuck asked.

Wes slopped the makings onto the bread and started to wrap it up. "Yeah, I got it," he said half-heartedly.

Chuck walked over. "Hey, how about making that a little neater?" he said exasperated.

"What does it matter? It's all goin' in the same place anyway."

"Trust me; it matters. Now straighten it up or make a new one," Chuck said shortly.

Wes gaped at him and rolled his eyes as he unwrapped the sub. The contents tumbled out in every direction. Wes shook his head and mumbled under his breath, "It's just a stupid sandwich. Like anyone cares what it looks like."

At the end of the night, Chuck approached Wes and announced, "Hey Wes, I need you to come in at two on Saturday. Melanie can't work on Saturday, and Dwayne can't get here until six. Can I count on you?"

Wes looked at him. "But I'm not supposed to come in until four."

"I know, but I'm short-handed, and I need you to come in earlier," Chuck said as he made notes on the schedule.

"Why can't Melanie work?" Wes asked in frustration.

Chuck stopped writing on the clipboard and turned to Wes. "She had a family function to go to. She asked for that time off."

"Fine," Wes said flatly and walked away. He could feel Chuck watching him, but he didn't care. It wasn't that he had plans on Saturday afternoon, but he didn't want to have to come in early either. *This place is such a joke,* he thought.

The next week, when Wes arrived at work, he noticed a new face. "Wes, this is Trey. He's new." Wes smiled and said his hellos. The guy looked nice enough.

As his shift wore on, Wes noticed Trey working really hard. He swept and mopped the floors, straightened the vegetable bins, scrubbed the soda dispenser, and unpacked new supplies. "Hey man, slow down. This isn't a marathon," Wes said.

"I just don't like standing around. I like to keep moving," Trey said as he went to wipe down the dining area tables.

After working a couple of shifts together, Wes noticed that Trey's zeal hadn't let up. Trey still outworked everyone else. *Knock yourself out,* Wes laughed inwardly.

The following week, when Wes reviewed the upcoming schedule, he noticed that he'd only been scheduled three nights instead of his standard five. *Cool,* he thought, *Finally, I can get out of this place.*

Though he enjoyed his down time, he felt frustrated when his paycheck came. It was almost half of what it had been. *Oh man,* he thought, *now how am I going to have enough money for gas and going out?*

Over the next few weeks, his scheduled hours decreased even more. One week, he was down to two nights and only a couple of hours on Saturday. What was going on? Frustrated, he approached Chuck about it. "Hey Chuck, why haven't I been getting more hours lately? I need to work."

Chuck gave him a small smile. "I thought you'd be happy to be working less. It doesn't seem like you want to be here anyway," he said.

"What's that supposed to mean?" Wes challenged. "I'm here when I'm supposed to be."

"Yeah, you're here. But you're either complaining or doing barely enough to get by. You don't take pride in your work; you throw the sandwiches together. You're short with the customers, and I have to *ask* for you to do anything extra," Chuck said flatly.

Wes looked away as his face started to turn red. As much as he hated to admit it, everything Chuck had said was true. He never put himself into his work.

"Look, Wes, I know this is just a job to you, but I need people who want to be here. I need people who want to work and have good attitudes while they're doing it."

"Are you firing me?" Wes asked in shock as the thought of getting fired gripped his stomach.

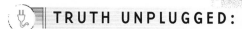 **TRUTH UNPLUGGED:**

Don't let a bad attitude ruin your relationships with your family, coworkers, or friends. Trust God to help you gain a more positive outlook on life.

"Not yet, but if you don't want to be here, then you need to go somewhere else. To be honest, I need people who are more like Trey. He comes in on time. He's pleasant, and he works hard. And he doesn't give me an attitude if I ask him to do something extra—like come in early. Right now, it's your choice. You can stay and work yourself up from the bottom of the list, or you can go."

Wes shrugged, "I'll keep working." After Chuck had walked away, Wes felt like he'd been punched in the stomach. How embarrassing would it have been to be fired for a bad attitude? His parents would have flipped at that. And how would he have responded at a future interview when someone asked him why he'd left the Sub Shack? That would have been awful.

Thankfully, he still had a job, but he wasn't going to make much money now since he was only getting the leftover hours. He had to start fresh and get busy. Turning to the preparation station, he noticed the tomato bin was low. Heading back to the large refrigerator, he decided, *I'd better make my time count.*

TRUTH LINK:

Dear Lord, I have really been frustrated lately about things in my life. Help me to deal with the situations with a good attitude. Sometimes I just can't help letting my irritation show. Help me to control my attitude and to have the wisdom to deal with what I need to do. Amen.

POWER UP:

Have you ever been accused of a bad attitude? Do you some-times think people just don't understand? It's true. People may not always understand what's troubling you, but be careful about allowing your concerns or irritations to continually flow onto others.

Put yourself in their place; would you want to be around someone who is constantly in a bad mood? What would you even-tually think about that person? Even if the person doesn't voice a bad attitude, it is usually obvious. If you're struggling to have a positive attitude, ask God to help you, and read your Bible. Not only will it give you great perspective on your life, but it will also remind you of all the things you have to be thankful for.

THE NEW PECKING ORDER

Persecution

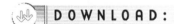 **DOWNLOAD:**

That is why, for Christ's sake, I delight in weaknesses, in insults, in hardships, in persecutions, in difficulties. For when I am weak, then I am strong. 2 Corinthians 12:10 NIV

Ted looked at his reflection in the mirror. He knew he was asking for trouble by wearing the T-shirt, but he didn't care. He felt nervous about boldly displaying his newfound faith; but in his mind, if it made him uncomfortable, that was just one more reason to do it.

"Hey honey, do you want some oatmeal for breakfast?" his mother asked when he walked into the kitchen. Then seeing his shirt, she smiled. "Nice shirt."

Ted knew his mother was happy with his decision to trust God with his life. They had attended church regularly since he was a small child, but it had only been within the last few months that he committed his life to Jesus.

Until now, you could have described him as more than a little wild. He had partied with the best of them, drinking his friends under the table and juggling several girls at one time; but when he prayed the prayer of salvation, his life changed. He knew that he had been headed down a bad road, but now he felt his heart had been changed and life had new purpose. There was something really comforting about knowing that Jesus had died for him and had accepted him in spite of the things he'd done.

This past weekend, he had attended a Christian concert with some of his friends from church. It was there that he bought his T-shirt. He had thought that when he became a Christian, he would have to give up good music, but he discovered that wasn't true. He found some great Christian bands who played more than just Gospel or Top 40 style.

Ted was still nervous about wearing his shirt in front of the guys he used to party with, since they had been ribbing him about his decision. Most of them knew he went to church. He had even invited them to come with him. They let him know that he was just going through a phase and that he'd be back, ready to raid their parents' liquor cabinets and pounce on the girls who frequented their parties.

As Ted was walking into the locker room to change for gym class later that morning, Randy Marshall called over to him. "Hey Ted, some of us are having a party out at Benson Lake. Wanna come?"

"Thanks, but I can't," Ted replied. Benson Lake was one of the many party spots in town. On any given weekend, there was always a keg of beer there.

Randy looked at him as if he felt sorry for him. "You're really taking this 'new creature thing' a little far, aren't you?" Then giving Ted's shirt a once over, he frowned and said, "You're turning into a regular Bible thumper. It's sad."

Ted noticed that other guys in the locker room were listening to their conversation. They pretty much fell into two groups. One looked at him like he'd just crawled out from under a rock, and the other avoided making eye contact at all. He didn't respond to Randy's comments; instead, he changed and lined up for gym class.

At lunch, he joined some of his friends. "I don't know if you can be seen with us, Father Ted," one of the guys sneered. "If lightning strikes our table, you really wouldn't want to get caught here." The group laughed.

Then another spoke up, "I really don't know if we can have you sit here with that shirt on, man. It's embarrassing and bad for our image." Again, laughter.

Ted moved to another table where he spent the rest of the lunch period alone. He didn't want to lose his old friends; he'd known them for

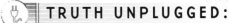

TRUTH UNPLUGGED:

People are watching you. Some will persecute you, but stand strong. You may be the only Bible some of those people will ever see. Make sure they see Jesus living in you.

years. He'd always had fun with them. But lately, the ribbing had gotten worse. He didn't know if he was a reminder that they weren't living right or if it was just the pecking order. He was different now, so logically, he was the one they targeted.

The rest of the day, he heard a few other chuckles and comments as he walked through the halls. The name "Father Ted" had obviously stuck.

In his last class, he arrived a few minutes early and took his seat. In front of him, a guy named Leon turned around and stared at him. Leon was more than a little different. His all-black wardrobe was some odd mix between Gothic and Rastafarian. His eyes were as black as his clothes, and he hid them behind huge dark-rimmed glasses. Ted had always found him a bit intimi-dating. He reminded Ted of a kid who might go postal in the school cafeteria one day. Unfortunately, they had assigned seats, so Ted couldn't get away from him.

Leon finally spoke in a slow, depressed tone. "You really believe that?" he said nodding toward Ted's shirt.

"Yeah, I do. Jesus changed my life."

"How'd He do that? He died eons ago."

"He died, but then He rose from the dead. I believe He's in Heaven talking to God about me and you and everyone else. I don't know how to explain it, but when I finally became a Christian, it was like a light came on. Thing just made sense."

After Ted finished, Leon remained quiet, as though he was really considering what Ted had said. When he finally spoke, he said simply, "That must be cool."

Then, the teacher started class and Leon turned around in his seat. Ted stared at the back of his head wondering. *Maybe wearing the shirt wasn't such a bad idea. Sure, I've had to deal with the comments and cheap shots that my friends have taken, but I wouldn't have had a chance to talk to Leon either.*

At the end of class, Ted waited for Leon outside the door. "Hey Leon, my church group is going to have a cookout and play softball this Saturday. You're welcome to come."

Leon looked surprised. "Um, let me think about it, okay?"

Ted said he'd talk to him later in the week and then walked back to his locker.

"Father Ted, I have a confession," one of his friends yelled down the hall.

Ted just rolled his eyes. Somehow the teasing didn't seem like such a big deal anymore.

TRUTH LINK:

Dear Lord, I want to stand strong for You; but I find it difficult to stand up when people pick on me, put me down, and call me names. Show me how to respond to the cheap shots people take. Give me just the words to say to everyone, the ones who pick on me and the ones who need to hear about You. Amen.

 POWER UP:

Have you ever found it difficult to stand up for what you believe? Maybe you're the only Christian in your school or at least the only one who really lives what you believe. If so, you know it's difficult when people pick on you for your beliefs or put you down in front of others.

Don't let them stop you from living your life for God. Being a Christian doesn't mean things will automatically be easy, but it does mean that you're on the winning team. Though it may be difficult, stay strong. Though you may only hear the negative, you'll never know whose life you may influence because of your faith.

DIRT, COBWEBS, AND MORE DIRT

Faithfulness

To the faithful you show yourself faithful, to the blameless you show yourself blameless. 2 Samuel 22:26 NIV

"Nicholas, have you taken Mrs. Jenkins' trash out to the curb yet?" his mother called from the kitchen.

"No, but I'm going to," Nicholas called back. He just needed a few more minutes on his computer to beat the game he was playing.

For the last two years, he had been helping their next door neighbor, Mrs. Jenkins, with chores around her house. She paid him to take out her trash, mow her lawn, weed her flowerbeds, and do other odd jobs around her house. She didn't pay much, but usually, Nicholas didn't mind. She was in her seventies and a widow. Her kids lived far away, and, most of the time, Nicholas was happy to help. She always made homemade cookies or lemonade for him. She'd sit with him and ask him all about his life—his friends, schoolwork, church, and whatever other topic came up. In return, she told him stories about her life when she was growing up.

After beating his game, Nicholas went over to Mrs. Jenkins' house. "Mrs. Jenkins, do you have any other trash you need me to take out?" he asked through her side screen door.

"My heavens, Nicholas. You startled me." She stood in her kitchen chopping carrots. Nicholas didn't know what she was cooking, but it sure smelled good. "Well, come in. I'm just finishing up this stew. I think there may be some trash in the bathroom that needs to go out."

Nicholas made his way through her compact house. Her furniture was slightly tattered from years of use, but everything was neat and clean. Photo frames filled with images of her grandchildren and great-grandchildren covered several surfaces. Nicholas always found himself very at home there. Though he didn't know from firsthand experience, he imagined it was just as a grandmother's home should be—comfortable and inviting.

After emptying the trash in the bathroom, he moved over to a stack of newspapers that were lying in the living room. "Mrs. Jenkins, do you want me to grab these newspapers too?" he asked.

"Yes, please. I finished reading those this morning," she responded.

After emptying the trash, Nicholas came back to her kitchen. "Do you need me to do anything else?"

"Actually, I wanted to talk to you about cleaning out my garage. It's full of stuff I haven't seen in years," she said motioning him to have a seat at her kitchen table.

Ugh! Nicholas thought. *That place is a rat trap.*

He'd been to the edge of her detached garage before, but he couldn't get in very far because every available space was filled, floor to ceiling, with all sorts of things: furniture, dirt, boxes, dirt, trunks, cobwebs, and more dirt. "When did you need it done?" he asked lamely.

"Well, I thought this weekend would be a good time since it'll probably take you a couple of days." His face must have shown his apprehension because she leaned over and patted his hand, "Don't worry, Nicholas, hard work never killed anybody."

Later at home, he complained to his mother about Mrs. Jenkins' request. She smiled and nodded. "That is going to be a big job, but I have confidence in you."

"Mom," he said, trying not to whine, "I can't do that. Do you know how long that will take me? That place should be torched, not cleaned."

She laughed. He knew he was being dramatic, but he couldn't think of a worse torture than cleaning out Mrs. Jenkins' garage.

"Sorry, Nicholas," his mother said with a smile, "you said you'd do it. So you have to stick to your word."

On Saturday, Nicholas dragged himself over to Mrs. Jenkins' house. He'd tried to think of every possible excuse to get out of doing it. He was even tempted to play sick, but he knew he couldn't lie to her.

Standing on her porch, Mrs. Jenkins gave him an enthusiastic wave. "Good morning, Nicholas. I have juice and muffins for you before you start." He gave her a weak smile, but he lacked enthusiasm for the task ahead.

After breakfast, he stood at the garage opening. It was just as he had remembered it. Mrs. Jenkins buzzed around him, giving instruction about how to sort what would eventually crawl out. "Let's place the furniture in the driveway. Place the boxes and trunks by the house. Put any tools against the wall, and anything else can go in the backyard. I'll sort while you pull everything out. Then I'll decide what to keep, what to give away, and what to throw away. Okay? Let's get started."

Nicholas began to pull things out one piece at a time. Within minutes, he felt like he needed another shower. Each time he moved a piece, dust whirled into the air. Some things he couldn't even identify because of the encrusted dirt. By midmorning, he was hot and caked with dirt too. Mrs. Jenkins was busy going through boxes and organizing things by what she would do with each piece.

Taking a break to enjoy a glass of iced tea, Nicholas looked at the garage. It looked like he'd barely made a dent. *This is going to take forever,* he thought.

The rest of the day passed with only short breaks for lunch and an afternoon snack. By the end of the day, Nicholas could see they were making headway. He could almost see the wall at the back of the garage.

He returned to work on Sunday following church. By three o'clock the garage had been emptied. Following another short break, he returned to work, hosing dirt

TRUTH UNPLUGGED:

To become a faithful person, be a person of your word, one others can count on.

off of tools and brushing dirt off of furniture. Mrs. Jenkins had efficiently sorted through the items and decided what needed to be put back in an orderly fashion. After deciding the best way to arrange the items, Nicholas began to refill the garage. He finished well after dark. Though there was still a lot in the garage, Mrs. Jenkins would be able to get in and out of the garage and tell what was what.

Pulling the garage door down, Nicholas felt exhausted. Turning, he saw Mrs. Jenkins coming his way, "Nicholas, I can't tell you how happy I am. I've needed to clean that out since my husband died fifteen years ago, but I knew I couldn't do it alone. Once again, you came through when I needed you. Now, I know I usually pay you one price for jobs like this, but I'd like to give you this instead."

Nicholas accepted the check she held out to him. He couldn't believe the amount, five hundred dollars. "Mrs. Jenkins, I can't take this," he stammered. "It's too much."

"Hogwash. You earned it," she said shortly. "I haven't seen anyone work that hard in years." Then she added with a smile, "And you never complained. I couldn't be more proud if you were my own grandson."

Nicholas walked home, took a shower, and collapsed into bed. He couldn't believe Mrs. Jenkins had given him so much or that he'd worked so hard. Drifting into a deep, deep sleep, Nicholas realized that Mrs. Jenkins hadn't rewarded him for the last two days alone. It was because he'd been faithful to help her so many others times as well, always with a good attitude.

Hmm—Maybe hard work isn't so bad after all.

TRUTH LINK:

Dear Lord, help me to be faithful in my life—with my relationships, my friends, and my work. Help me to give my all in whatever I do so people know they can depend on me. Amen.

POWER UP:

Are you the kind of person people can count on—in good times and in bad? Are you someone people know they can turn to because you always come through for them? Becoming a faithful person doesn't begin with big choices. Instead, it starts with small things—doing chores, keeping confidences, helping friends in need.

When you think about the kind of person you want to be, of course, you want to be someone others can count on, someone who is faithful. So start where you are and make the decision to finish what you say you'll do, in the time you say you'll do it, with the quality others expect. Then you will be well on your way to becoming a faithful person, someone whom God will reward.

GET OUTTA MY LIFE!

Sibling Rivalry

 **DOWNLOAD:**

Love is patient, love is kind. It does not envy, it does not boast, it is not proud. It is not rude, it is not self-seeking, it is not easily angered, it keeps no record of wrongs. Love does not delight in evil but rejoices with the truth. It always protects, always trusts, always hopes, always perseveres. Love never fails.

1 Corinthians 13:4-8 NIV

"Where's my leather jacket?" Eric demanded as he stormed into the kitchen, glaring at his brother who sat at the breakfast table enjoying a bowl of cereal.

"I don't know," Elton responded.

"I know you have it. It was in my closet last week, and now it's gone. I haven't worn it, and you're the only other person who would wear it. Hand it over," Eric barked.

"I don't have your stupid leather jacket!"

"Mom, tell him to give me my leather jacket," Eric called to his mother who stood in the nearby utility room, emptying clothes from the washing machine and putting them into the dryer.

"I don't have it, you jerk!" Elton yelled back.

"Boys, stop yelling. Eric, your brother said he doesn't have it. Elton, finish your breakfast. You're both going to be late for school if you don't hurry," their mother said.

"I can't believe you believe him. You always take his side," Eric yelled, storming out of the kitchen.

For as long as he could remember, Eric had dealt with his younger brother's irritations. They were only eighteen months apart in age, and he couldn't remember a time when Elton wasn't there. Eric felt that their mother always took Elton's side because he was the youngest. It seemed like Elton could do no wrong; whereas Eric was older and had to be more responsible. That was what his mother had said, and Eric was sick of it.

School was the only place Eric got relief from his brother. There, they were in different grades—two years apart—and had different friends. Eric hung out with his friends on the basketball teams, while Elton was on the soccer team. Their paths didn't cross very often.

"Hey Eric, can I get a ride home from school with you?" Elton asked in the hallway between classes. "Mom can't pick me up, and she told me to ride with you."

"No, I have basketball practice until four. Find another ride," Eric said.

Elton looked frustrated. "Come on, Eric, I need a ride. I'll wait."

"I said no."

"Why do you always act like such a jerk? Like I ever did anything to you," Elton responded.

"Give me a break," Eric shot back. "You're always in my business. I swear I wish you would just get outta my life." Then turning, he stormed away.

After school Eric attended basketball practice and then took his friend Sheldon home. When he walked in the door, the house was quiet. Eric got a drink from the kitchen before sitting down to do his homework at the kitchen table. At 6:30, his mother walked in the door with her arms full of bags.

"Will you and your brother help me unload the groceries?" his mother asked as she set the first load on the counter.

"Sure, I will. I don't know where Elton is," Eric said, closing his trigonometry book and rising to go out the garage door.

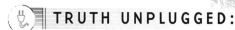 **TRUTH UNPLUGGED:**

Your brothers and sisters need as much or more kindness, love, mercy, and patience from you as anyone else you meet.

"What do you mean you don't know where he is?" his mother asked, turning to face him. "Didn't he come home with you?"

"No," Eric shrugged, "he got another ride."

"I told him to get a ride with you. What happened?"

Eric huffed, "I told him I had practice and he needed to get another ride."

His mother stared at him with wide eyes. "You refused to give your brother a ride? It's 6:30, he's still not home, and you stand there with an attitude? Get on the phone right now and find your brother." His mother sounded tense. Eric could tell she was on the verge of losing her temper.

Eric huffed again and stalked to the phone, dialing Elton's best friend. After five phone calls, he still didn't know where Elton was. After ten phone calls, he started to run out of ideas and began to worry. Where was Elton? Why hadn't he found a ride and come straight home?

"Any news?" his mother asked, glancing at the clock. It was 7 P.M.

"No, several people say they saw him after school, but no one could give him a ride home. They haven't seen him since," Eric answered.

"I'm going to look for him," his mother said, grabbing her keys and heading out the door. "Call your father and let him know."

Eric continued to phone anyone who could possibly know where Elton was. If he hadn't been so mean, Elton would have been home hours ago. Now, his mother was out frantically looking for him. "God, please bring my brother home safe. I'm sorry I was a jerk to him. I'll do better; just please bring him home," he prayed.

At 7:30 his mother walked in with Elton. "Thank God. Where have you been?" Eric asked in desperate relief.

"I was at the school helping Ms. Watson with the signs for the game this weekend. She said she'd bring me home after we finished since I didn't have a ride. Time just got away from me," Elton said.

"We'll talk about it later. I'll call your dad and let him know you're okay. Right now, I want you to go unload your stuff and clean up for dinner. I want to talk to your brother," their mother said. After Elton left the kitchen, she sat down at the table and motioned for Eric to join her. "Eric, it has to stop."

"What?" Eric said, though he had a good idea as to where this was going.

"You are so angry at your brother all the time. You don't even see him as a person. And today, your actions could have had serious consequences. Now, Elton is responsible for not calling to tell me where he was, but he wouldn't have had to look for another ride if you hadn't refused to give him one when he asked you. You are *not* the only one in this family."

Eric looked down at the table. "I know, Mom, but he's always in my way. And you always take his side on things. School is the only place I can get away from him."

"That's true," his mother nodded. "But it's also the only place he can get away from you. And I don't always take his side on things, but honestly, you blow up so fast whenever it comes to your brother that I try to smooth things over rather than let him catch it from both of us. You have zero patience when it comes to him. He's not perfect, but neither are you. You need to ease up."

Eric nodded reluctantly.

"And by the way, I found your leather jacket that you were so sure your brother had taken. It was in the back of my car. You forgot it when we went out for pizza last week." After watching him a few seconds, his mother rose to prepare dinner.

Eric continued to stare at the table. He felt ashamed. He really had been cruel to his brother. Sure Elton could be irritating, but maybe he had been just as irritating at his brother's age.

Thanks for bringing him home safe, God, he prayed silently as he rose to set the table. *Just like I promised, I'll make more of an effort to be nice to him.*

TRUTH LINK:

Dear Lord, please help me to show Your love—Your grace, Your mercy, Your kindness—to my brothers and sisters. Help me to be the best brother I can be. Amen.

 ## POWER UP:

Have you ever noticed how difficult it is to show the love of God to your brothers and sisters? It's true. They can get into your stuff and razz you over the littlest things. They know just which buttons to push to make you angry—and they push them better than anyone.

Showing them patience and kindness can be hard, but well worth it. As irritating as they may be, remember no one can ever take their place. You understand each other better than most because you've grown up in the same family, regardless of whether you're full, half, or step siblings. In time, hopefully, you'll be able to celebrate each other's victories and talents, instead of focusing on each other's failures and weaknesses.

WE'RE IN THIS TOGETHER

Illness

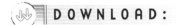
"Mick, are you going to the hospital to visit your mother today?" his father asked. Mick noticed how tired he looked. Dark circles shadowed his eyes, and his shoulders slumped in a way they never had before.

"I don't know. I'll have to see," Mick said before heading out the door to his job.

His mother had recently had surgery and treatment for cancer. Since then, Mick's dad had practically lived at the hospital. Every day he asked if Mick would go to the hospital too, and every day Mick said he'd have to wait and see. Mick knew he should visit more often, but he just couldn't. He couldn't stand to see his mother so sick and weak. She'd lost her hair and quite a bit of weight. She had a pale, ghostly look. Mick almost didn't recognize her.

He remembered vividly how his parents had sat him down to tell him she was sick. "Mick, the doctors found a lump in my breast. They've done a biopsy, and it's malignant. I have to go into the hospital for a mastectomy and chemotherapy treatment. Now, I don't want you to worry. We'll get through this," she had said so calmly, but Mick knew the truth. She had been standing strong for his dad and him.

As she spoke, Mick noticed his father staring off with a blank look on his face. He'd always been a strong, larger-than-life sort of guy, but Mick sensed that he was struggling. Mick knew it wasn't as simple as his mother had made it sound. The only thing he had known about cancer was that his grandmother had died of it years ago, but Mick had been young enough that all he could remember was his mother crying after she died. When she broke the news of her own illness, his mother looked healthy, strong, and fit. At the time, Mick couldn't fathom that she was sick. She looked so normal.

The day of her surgery, he and his dad sat with her until she was wheeled into the operating room. She made jokes, trying to ease the tension, but Mick couldn't be soothed. He watched as a procession of people from their church visited. Several tried to console him with their words like: "God knows best" or "She's in God's hands now."

He hadn't wanted to hear what they said. In fact, the more they spoke, the angrier he became. They didn't understand what he was feeling. His mother had gone into surgery for *cancer,* such an ugly word. She was his mother. She didn't belong to them. They didn't know her like he did. They didn't love her like he did. They couldn't possibly have known what was going through his mind.

Since the surgery had been expected to take quite a while, he decided to take a walk. He couldn't just sit in the waiting room as the walls closed in around him. But walking up and down the halls didn't help either. He saw all kinds of sick people and smelled all sorts of strange, strong, clinical smells. All of it made his skin crawl. Inwardly, he screamed, *God, why did this happen? Why is my mother going through this?* And then he begged, *Please help her. Please don't let her die.*

After the surgery, he and his dad sat in her room. He watched his dad stroke her hand. He'd always known his parents loved each other. They had been affectionate around the house and, much to Mick's embarrassment, had still gone on dates. But as he watched his dad, he saw how difficult this was for him. Seeing his father in such pain only intensified his own.

TRUTH UNPLUGGED:

When an illness strikes your family, God can give you courage and strength to face the situation. Ask Him.

Then they found another tumor under his mother's arm, causing her to have a second surgery. After that, Mick had only visited the hospital once. He was shocked by his mother's appearance. Since then, he hadn't been back. He just couldn't take it.

Driving to his job, he began to pray again for his mother, "Lord, please heal my mother. Please let the surgery and treatment work, so she can come home and be strong again." As he prayed the same words that he'd prayed a hundred times every day since she told him the news, he felt strange. He pulled his car into a parking lot. Then, as if a dam broke, he wept for the first time. He let it all go—all the pain and all the fear. He wasn't sure how long he sat there, but finally his tears began to dry up, and he knew what he had to do.

Turning his car around, he headed to the hospital. Like a robot, he walked through the lobby, entered the elevator, and pushed the button to her floor. He smelled the same smells, but he didn't stop. For the first time, he wasn't afraid. Entering her room, he stopped. She was still so small, but he didn't let the sight of her scare him. *She's my mom,* he repeated over and over again in his head.

Walking to the side of her bed, he took a seat and gently took his mother's hand. She opened her eyes, focused on him, and smiled. "Hey there."

"Hey Mom," he said with tears in his eyes. "How are you feeling today?"

"I'm actually feeling better today," she responded slowly, closing her eyes.

"It's okay, Mom," he said. "You sleep. I'm here, and Dad's coming. We're going to get through this, you hear? We're all in this together."

He watched as she gently nodded her head and drifted off to sleep.

Still holding her hand, he bowed his head and began to pray, "Okay Lord, I'm here, and I'm not leaving. I need her to be healed and home with Dad and me. And just like I know You haven't given up on her, I haven't either, and I'm not going to."

For the first time, he felt the courage and determination to make good on his prayer. He realized that what he'd said to his mother was true; this was a family thing—the hardest they'd ever faced—but they were all in it together.

TRUTH LINK:

Dear Lord, I have a loved one who is ill, and I need You to help us through this. I rely on You as the Healer—because I know You can and will heal. And as You work on my loved one's behalf, I pray You will also show me how to deal with this. Give me the wisdom, courage, and peace to handle this situation. Amen.

POWER UP:

When illness strikes your family, it affects everyone. If you've faced this, you know how true that statement is. Everyone does his or her best to handle the situation, but it's still difficult to know what to say or how to act. You may get angry or pull away, trying to deny that anything's wrong. Or you may feel depressed. You may turn into Superman, trying to handle everything that needs to be done.

Whatever the situation, take time to pray. Lean on Jesus to show you what to do and how to handle things. Ask Him for healing, strength, and courage. You're not alone; He's right there with you.

GETTING THE WHOLE STORY

Criticism

DOWNLOAD:

Those people are on a dark spiral downward. But if you think that leaves you on the high ground where you can point your finger at others, think again. Every time you criticize someone, you condemn yourself. Romans 2:1

"Hey, Jake, where's the popcorn? We're ready to start the movie," Logan called from the living room where Jake's closest friends were gathered for their Friday night movie-fest.

"It's coming. What does everyone want to drink?" he called back. "And who wants to help me get them?"

Marcy jumped up and ran to the kitchen. "I'll help. By the way, is John coming?"

"You know him, he's always late," Jake said.

Jake and Marcy carried trays of sodas, popcorn, and chips into the living room where everyone grabbed their favorite spots. Jake sat on the floor leaning on a big pillow. Logan stretched out in the recliner. Marcy and David took the couch. That only left John, who usually sprawled out on the floor. They were all set for their *Indiana Jones* marathon.

"Should we wait for John?" Logan asked.

"Yeah, let's give him a few minutes," David piped up. "He should be here anytime."

"You guys, he's *always* late. We shouldn't wait on him," Jake reasoned, grabbing a handful of popcorn. "Now that he's got that new pizza delivery job, you just can't count on him. He should have gotten off thirty minutes ago, but with him, you just can't tell."

"I don't think he's *always* late," Marcy said, eyeing Jake. "He just needs a little more time to get here since he's working now. We have time; let's wait."

Jake shrugged.

He didn't necessarily mind waiting for John, but it irked him that he wasn't there when he knew they always started the movies at 9:00 P.M. They had been meeting for Friday night movies for the last year. Each week, they voted on the movie for the following Friday, and if they couldn't decide, they drew titles out of a hat. It had been running smoothly until John got his job. His new schedule really threw a wrench into their get-togethers.

After about five minutes, Jake grew impatient. He went to the phone and dialed John's number. "Are you coming?" he barked into the receiver when John answered his cell phone.

"I'm on my way right now. I had a big delivery out on South Pine Street. I should be there in ten minutes," he explained.

"Fine. Just get here. We're waiting," he said into the phone before quickly hanging up.

Turning to the group, he found Marcy glaring at him. "Ease up, Jake. It's not like Indiana Jones is going anywhere."

Jake shook his head and took a seat on the floor again. "It just bugs me that he knows we start at nine and he's still not here.

This has happened a lot lately." He didn't care what Marcy said. In his opinion, John's lateness was getting out of hand.

The other day, John was supposed to have met him at the movies at 6 P.M., but he didn't show up until 6:20. Then he was supposed to have given him a ride to the hockey game last week, and he was thirty minutes late. They missed the first goal. It was becoming a habit, and Jake didn't feel he could count on John anymore. Although John always apologized and even called to say he'd be late, Jake didn't care. John was supposed to be there when he said he would be there; it was as simple as that.

Ten minutes later, John walked in carrying a pizza. "Sorry, I'm late. I brought a pizza." He set it down on the kitchen table and collapsed onto the floor. "I'm so tired," he said. "We had a huge delivery out on South Pine Street. It took two cars to get it all there. I was supposed to get off an hour ago, but they needed me to help. I got a good tip though."

Jake went to the kitchen to grab paper plates and napkins for the pizza. Though he was always happy to have pizza, he was still irritated that John was late. As he placed everything on the table, the others talked about this and that: their days, John's job, the movie, the pizza, and other inconsequential things. Jake didn't join in their conversation; he was too angry.

"Pizza's ready," he called with a slight edge in his voice.

Everyone poured into the kitchen, grabbing paper plates and napkins. Jake waited for everyone to get theirs before getting his. Back in the living room, they all took their spots when Jake spoke up, "Do we still have time for the movie, or do we need to choose something shorter?" he asked.

Everyone looked at one another and then at him. "I think we have plenty of time," Marcy piped up.

"Fine. Start it," Jake responded flatly.

Irritated, he drained his cola and rose to get a refill. In the kitchen, John joined him. "What's your problem, man? Why are you so angry?"

Slamming the freezer door, he turned on him. "My problem? My problem is that I'm tired of always waiting for you. You know we start the movies at nine. Why can't you be on time anymore?"

"I'm sorry. What else do you want me to say? I have a job now. I can't always control when I get off," he reasoned with tension in his voice.

"I don't *care* about your job," he said.

"Well, you may not, but I do. I'm not like you, Jake. My parents don't pay for everything. I have to work. If I don't keep this job, my parents will take my car away."

 TRUTH UNPLUGGED:

Compassion from you may be the tool God wants to use to help someone in need.

Jake stood there stunned.

He realized that he had never bothered to find out why John worked so hard. He thought John just liked the extra money his job provided. Now, he felt like a jerk. He'd been so self-righteous about John being late because he assumed that he and John were dealing with the same things. Now, he realized there were special circumstances. "I'm sorry, man. I didn't know," he said quietly.

"Yeah, well, I don't advertise it. Most of what I make goes to pay for my car, so I sometimes try to pick up extra shifts to have spending money," he said. Jake nodded, finally understanding. John peeked around the corner at the television screen and then looked back at Jake, "Come on, let's go watch the movie. I promise I'll try to be on time from now on."

"Good." Jake smiled. "And I promise to ease up and not be so critical."

John punched him on the shoulder lightly, "Great. Come on, let's go eat some pizza and watch Indie womp up on the Nazis."

With the remaining pieces of pizza in hand, they returned to the living room, took their seats, and enjoyed the rest of the movie among their best friends.

TRUTH LINK:

Dear Lord, please forgive me for being critical of others. I know I need to be understanding and realize that I may not know everything about certain situations or people. Please help me to be compassionate and understanding. Amen.

POWER UP:

Have you ever found yourself being critical of someone else—maybe a friend, a sibling, or even a complete stranger? Perhaps you thought the person should act a certain way or do something that he or she was not doing.

When you criticize someone, you become that person's judge, but you may not necessarily have all the facts. Maybe the person is in a no-win situation and is handling things the best way he or she knows how. Or maybe there's more to the story than you have been told. Or maybe the person is responding to something based on past experience.

Regardless of the reason, the individual needs your understanding. That's not to say that if the person is in sin, you should condone it. You shouldn't. But instead of becoming critical, take your concerns to God in prayer. Then ask Him to help you be the best friend, witness, or family member you can be. Your understanding may be a tool God uses to help a person in need.

GOT IT PRETTY GOOD

Thankfulness

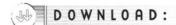 **DOWNLOAD:**

Let the peace of Christ keep you in tune with each other, in
step with each other. . . . And cultivate thankfulness.

Colossians 3:15

"Man, my dad is driving me crazy!" Heath said in frustration.
He'd just come from his house where he'd had another fight with his
dad. "He just won't get off my back about school. He actually said
I need to get a tutor for the SATs this summer. Isn't that crazy?"

"Why does he think you need a tutor?" Myles asked as he bent
over the engine of his car. He continued working on it as Heath
ranted about his dad, something he often did.

"He's not sure I'll make high enough scores on my own to get
into Wellington. They require a 1200. Like I care about going to
Wellington," he said pacing back and forth across the garage. "He
just hounds me all the time. Why can't he just lay off?"

"Do you think you can get a high enough score on your own?" Myles asked.

"I don't know. I just know I don't want to study this summer. I want a real summer. I want to go on one of those outdoor adventure treks. Ya know those hiking, mountain climbing, and camping tours. My dad says he'll only pay for it if I get a tutor for the rest of the summer. It stinks!"

When Myles didn't respond, Heath looked down at what Myles was doing. Heath didn't know much about cars, but Myles did. He was always tinkering with or fixing his and his mother's cars. Heath usually just stood around handing him tools. Over the years, he'd come to recognize the difference between a Phillips and a flat-head screwdriver, but that's about it. "So you want to go grab a pizza and go to the batting cages?"

Myles peered out from under the hood. "Sounds like fun, but I've got stuff to do around the house this afternoon."

Considering what Myles had said for a minute, Heath offered, "What if I help you? We could get everything done fast and then go to the cages." Myles accepted Heath's plan, and they set out to finish Myles' list of chores as quickly as possible.

"Well, I need to mow and edge the lawn and trim the bushes," Myles said.

Heath had mowed at his house a few times and suggested that he start there. When Myles uncovered the push lawn mower, Heath scowled. "You mean you don't have a riding lawn mower?" Myles laughed in response and pushed it out to the driveway.

After checking the oil and the gas, he primed the motor, adjusted the choke, and started it in one swift jerk. Heath stood back the entire time, realizing that he was on foreign turf. He'd never had to do any of that. Most of the time, his father mowed the lawn. Occasionally, they even hired professionals to do it. Every once in a while Heath did it, but then all he had to do was sit on the back of a big riding lawn mower and turn a key. If it didn't start, he called his dad. No problem.

This was different.

As he began to push the mower around the yard, he noticed immediately that not only was the mower not a riding mower, but it didn't move easily. When they said push mower, they meant throw your back into it. Heath felt like he was doing continuous reps of leg presses as he pushed his weight against the machine, coaxing it to move.

After mowing, he moved on to the edging and trimming. Looking around, he didn't see Myles anywhere. Imagining that Myles was off loafing while Heath did his work for him, he went looking for him. As he wandered through Myles' house, he heard a noise from the master bedroom. Peaking around the corner, he saw Myles lying on the floor in the adjoining master bathroom. "What're you doing?" he asked.

"My mom said there's a leak under here. I think I almost have it fixed," Myles said as he strained to tighten the nut.

"Why don't you just call a plumber?" Heath asked in confusion.

Myles laughed as he continued to strain. "Cause—this—doesn't—cost—anything."

Heath left to return to the yard where he continued edging the sidewalk and trimming the bushes. As he worked,

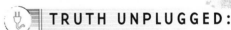 **TRUTH UNPLUGGED:**

Instead of looking at the things that aren't quite right in your life, focus on all the good things God has done for you.

he thought back to the difference between his life and Myles'. He'd never really considered it before. He knew that Myles' dad had left years before and that Myles hadn't had anything to do with him. He knew that Myles' mom worked in an office downtown as a secretary. Although Myles never complained, Heath knew money wasn't as easy to come by for them.

As far back as he could remember, Myles had worked. He'd mowed yards around the neighborhood when he wasn't old enough to get other work. Now, he worked for a landscape company before and after school and on weekends. Heath hadn't really thought about it before. He just figured Myles liked to work. Now, he wondered if Myles worked out of necessity instead of desire.

Wiping the sweat from his brow, he walked back into the house. "What next?" he asked, getting into the spirit of things.

"My mom wanted me to clean the windows and window screens. Once we do that, we should be finished," Myles said, looking around as if trying to remember if there was anything else.

Outside, they worked together. One removed the screens and washed them before returning them to their places. The other concentrated on cleaning the windows. As they worked, they talked about their upcoming senior year. "So, have you figured out where you're going to college?" Heath asked.

Myles was quiet for a while. "I'm not sure. If I go, it'll be to the community college."

"Community college?" Heath asked in surprise. "But you've got great grades. You can get into just about any school you want. Why stay at the community college?"

"I can get a scholarship, and I can still live here with my mom. I've already got a job, and my boss said he'll give me my own crew next year. So I'll make more money. I can help my mom out more. It just makes sense," he answered as he continued to work.

"But what about the whole college experience: living in the dorms, going to college games, dating college girls, all that?" Heath asked.

Myles shook his head. "That's not for me. I've got other things to think about: taking care of my mom, taking care of our house, making money. I don't have time for all that other stuff."

They continued working in silence. Heath couldn't believe how easy his life was by comparison. He and Myles had been friends for years, but he'd never acknowledged this side of Heath's life. He'd been too wrapped up in his own. He had never even considered not going to college. It was just a matter of which one. His dad wrote the checks.

Even now, he thought of the argument he'd had with his dad earlier, which seemed to pale in comparison to Myles' life. Heath's dad offered to send him on a two-week adventure trek that was surely going to cost a lot of money, but Heath had thrown a fit because his dad demanded that he first study to get into a top-notch university. All he had to do was make the grade; that was it. Other than that, his ticket was paid. *Wow,* he thought, *I really do have it pretty good.*

After they finished the windows, Heath was exhausted. He'd never worked so hard in his life. As they climbed into Myles' car, Heath turned to his friend, "You know, maybe we should just get the pizza and skip the batting cages. I don't think I could hit anything right now."

Myles laughed. "I think you're right. Thanks for helping me. You saved me a lot of time."

"No problem," Heath responded as they pulled out of the driveway, but inside he thought, *No, thank you. You're the one who's helped me.*

TRUTH LINK:

Dear Lord, please forgive me for taking all of the good things in my life for granted. Help me to see everything You've given me and done for me. Help me to keep an attitude of thankfulness. Amen.

POWER UP:

Do you ever catch yourself taking people or things for granted? Your family's love and advice? Opportunities? Choices you've been allowed to make? At one time or another, everyone forgets to look at the good things and instead focuses on the things that aren't so good.

But God wants you to be grateful for all the good He's put in your life. As you're thankful to Him and others around you, you'll be able to be a better example of His love to the world. And by focusing on all the good things in your life, you'll be able enjoy your blessings even more.

WATCH THAT MOUTH

Profanity

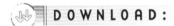 **DOWNLOAD:**

Guard your tongue from profanity, and no more lying through your teeth. Turn your back on sin; do something good. Embrace peace—don't let it get away! Psalm 34:13-14

"Pass me the ball!" Steve shouted at Rob. They were practicing hard for an upcoming game against their biggest rival. The outcome would determine which team moved into the district playoffs. "What are you waiting for?" Steve moved into position under the basket. When Rob attempted and missed a three-point shot, Steve erupted. "#@$&%!"

"Watch that mouth, Steve, or you'll be running sprints for the rest of practice," Coach Higgins yelled.

"But Coach, I was open," he yelled back. "He's just being a #@$&%!"

"You got some mouth on you," Coach Higgins said in response to Steve's angry outburst. Then pointing to the far end of the gym where the team ran sprints, he said, "Now, hit it!"

Steve left the rest of the team and jogged down to the far end of the gym, mumbling the entire way. "Keep it up, Steve, and you'll be warming the bench on Friday," Coach Higgins yelled after hearing Steve's continued protests.

After practice, Steve joined the rest of the team in the locker room. Finding Rob, he demanded an explanation. "What's your problem, man? I could have made that shot."

Rob turned and moved within inches of Steve's face, "You're *not* the *only* player on this team. I knew what I was doing. And the last thing I'm gonna do is give in to your big mouth," Rob said with a look of contained rage in his eyes.

Steve's anger was just as strong, but he held back. Rob might not have been the team's star basketball player, but Steve was pretty sure he could wipe the floor up with someone if he put his mind to it. And the look in his eyes confirmed that his mind was pretty well set on it right then.

"There are other people out there, ya know? We'll lose on Friday night if we all go solo," Steve continued to rant.

Rob sneered as he continued toward Steve, nose to nose, "Great advice. You walk around out there like you're some kind of god on the court and rail on everyone else when they miss a basket. You make me sick!" Realizing they were on the verge of coming to blows, Steve backed away and returned to his locker.

After he had changed, he stepped outside and found his best friend, Damon. "Could you believe Rob today?" he asked, shaking his head in disgust. He and Damon not only lived within a few blocks of each other, but they both had a passion for basketball.

"Rob? What about you? Since when do you cuss people out on the court?" Damon asked in amazement.

"What? He deserved it. That was a stupid move. You know if he pulls that on Friday, we'll lose."

Damon shook his head at Steve's response. "Man, you keep that up, and no one will want to play with you. You'll probably be kicked off the team," Damon said.

"I can speak my mind," Steve shot back.

Damon stopped walking. "Speaking your mind and cussing people out on the court are two different things."

For the rest of the week, Steve made a point to keep his comments to himself at practice, not that he didn't want to blast some of the other guys for their stupid mistakes. He was certain that if they didn't watch it, they would lose the game.

On Friday, Coach Higgins gathered everyone together for his usual pregame pep talk. "Okay everyone, settle down. I think we all know what's riding on this game. We've got a strong team, and you've worked hard. I have no doubt that if you want this game badly enough, you can win it. Remember, this is a team sport, and it takes a team to win. So no cowboying around out there. You're all in this together. Let's see what you can do." Everyone yelled, pumping themselves up for the game.

Out on the court, Steve took his place. He was ready. When the tip-off came, Steve launched into action. He worked to get away from the defense so he could take a shot, but he couldn't shake his defense. The guy was on him the whole time. He broke right, then left. He tried to fake the guy out, but nothing worked. While the rest of the team moved the ball down the court to shoot, Steve's defense covered him.

When a moment finally came for Steve to get a pass, the guy knocked it away before Steve could get a good hold. Angry, Steve shoved the guy. "You #@$&%, get off me!" As the guy fell to the ground, Steve heard the referee's whistle blow. He'd fouled the guy, allowing the other team to take two foul shots.

Steve looked around to find support from his teammates, but they were glaring back at him. *What's their problem?* he wondered in disgust.

Back in play, it was Steve's turn to guard his opponent. Hovering close without fouling him, Steve worked to keep the guy away from the ball. When the guy did get the ball, he faked left and ran right. Steve lost his footing and stumbled, allowing the guy to take a shot and win two more points for the other team.

Furious, Steve couldn't help getting in the guy's face. "You tripped me on purpose, you #@$&%!"

"Man, get outta my face. I didn't touch you. You fell over your own big feet."

"#@$&%!" Steve let lose a string of curses that could be heard all over the court. Just when he thought he would lose it with the guy, he again heard the referee's whistle blow.

Looking around, he saw his coach motioning him to the sidelines. "Take a seat," his coach said through clenched teeth when Steve arrived at the sidelines.

"You're pulling me out of the game?" Steve cried in surprise.

His coach turned to face him nose to nose. "You'll be lucky if I don't throw you off this team," he said in a slow menacing voice. Shocked, Steve sat down.

For the remainder of the game, Steve watched as his team and the opponent went head-to-head. First, his team would pull ahead, and then the other team would move up by two. At one point, one of his teammates had the ball stolen right before an important shot. Steve jumped to his feet, "You stupid . . . " Just when he was about to let the profanity fly, he saw the coach give him a look, almost daring him to finish the sentence. Catching himself, he quickly sat down.

Back and forth the two teams battled until the last two minutes of the game. It was then that Rob made a three-point shot, taking their team's lead to six points. Then Damon rebounded a shot and took it down the court for another two points, taking their lead to eight. As the clock ran out, Steve's team ran together and high-fived all over the court. Steve ran out to join the team. They were on their way to the district playoffs.

After showering and changing, Steve walked out of the locker room and into Coach Higgins. "Steve, I need to talk to you a minute." Steve followed him into his office. "You crossed a line out there tonight—several times—and I can't ignore it."

Steve looked at him confused. "What? So I lost my temper and said some things I shouldn't have said. I'm sorry. I'll do better."

His coach nodded and motioned for Steve to take a seat in the chair opposite his desk. "Steve, you're a good player and a good kid, but your mouth is out of control.

 **TRUTH UNPLUGGED:**

God has given you the skills, intelligence, and creativity to express yourself without using profanity.

You think you can say anything you want and then apologize afterwards and everything will be okay, but it isn't. Your language cost us valuable time and points out on the floor tonight. And more than that, I was embarrassed for you and for this team. And I won't have that. So you are suspended from this team for the rest of the year. I've warned you several times about your outbursts over the last few weeks. If you can clean up your act by next year, you can try out again. But don't even think about coming back on my court cussing like a sailor again. Are we clear?"

Steve sat stunned. "So I can't play in the playoffs? That's not fair!"

"I'll tell you what's not fair," the coach said, leaning across the desk. "It's not fair that the other players and I have to listen to your mouth. That's what's not fair. I thought maybe you would change. That's why I repeatedly gave you chances. But I think you've made it a habit, and sometimes it takes extreme measures to break a habit."

Steve left the coach's office feeling lower than he'd ever felt. He couldn't believe he'd been suspended from the team for the rest of the year. He was angry at Coach Higgins for taking such a tough stand, but more than anything, he was mad at himself for letting his language get so out of control that it cost him a chance to play in the district playoffs.

While the other players went out to celebrate at the local pizza joint, Steve drove home feeling very alone.

TRUTH LINK:

Dear Lord, help me to keep my words clean, free from profanity. I want to be a good example of how Your people should speak and act. Amen.

POWER UP:

Have you ever been around someone who curses incessantly? Sometimes people mistakenly think that using profanity makes you cool. They start to do it just to fit in, but before long, it becomes a habit. The truth is, using profanity says a lot about you. It says that you're unable, either because of a lack of education or creativity, to express yourself clearly with intelligent words. Basically, it debases you.

People—acquaintances, teachers, coaches, bosses, and coworkers—will judge you based on how you express yourself. And though you don't want to be ruled by others' opinions, you do have to realize that those people have the power to make your life easier or harder. And when it comes down to it, God has made you creative and intelligent and special. So determine not to use profanity; God has made you so much better than that.

BETTER THAN YOU CAN IMAGINE

Death

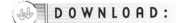

DOWNLOAD:

None of this fazes us because Jesus loves us. I'm absolutely convinced that nothing—nothing living or dead, angelic or demonic, today or tomorrow, high or low, thinkable or unthinkable—absolutely nothing can get between us and God's love because of the way that Jesus our Master has embraced us.

Romans 8:37-39

Dan sat in Terry's bedroom. He had to get away from all the people around the house. He still couldn't believe his best friend was dead. He told himself that Terry was gone, but his heart just couldn't believe it. Any minute he expected Terry to come into the room. "What's wrong with you?" he'd say. "Why waste this day inside? Let's go!"

That was Terry—adventurous, fun-loving, and upbeat. People always felt better when he was around.

What am I going to do? Dan wondered.

His family and friends tried to tell him that his feelings were normal, but they didn't *feel* normal. He was still in shock. At times he felt so angry that he just wanted to hit something. Why had Terry and his family gone on vacation to Florida? They never went on vacation, so why this year? And why had Terry gone into the ocean that morning by himself? Dan already knew the answer.

Terry had always been a strong swimmer, and there was nothing he loved more than swimming first thing in the morning. He'd been a lifeguard at the public pool, so there was no reason for him to doubt that he could handle swimming alone that morning. Unfortunately, he'd been wrong, horribly wrong. According to the Coast Guard, he went out too far and got caught in a heavy current from which he couldn't break free. It dragged him out to sea, drowning him along the way.

His parents had realized he was missing when he hadn't shown up for breakfast later that morning, but by that time, it was too late. He was already gone.

Dan continued to sit in Terry's bedroom. Looking around, he felt like Terry was still there. He saw the photos of Terry's family and friends—usually posing in some crazy, funny way. He noticed the swimming trophies and all the memorabilia that so many high school juniors have in their rooms. He looked at the set of drums Terry had played. Then he saw the worn Bible that sat on Terry's dresser.

Walking over to it, Dan picked it up. Terry loved the Bible. He was passionate about God—pure and simple. The previous summer, Terry had invited Dan to attend church camp. "Trust me; you'll love it!" Terry had promised, and he'd been right. Dan had been shocked to find that something church related was so much fun.

During that camp, Dan received Christ and dedicated his life to Him. If it hadn't been for Terry, he never would have discovered how fulfilling and rewarding life as a Christian could be.

Before he became a Christian, he had very little hope in his life. He felt depressed and angry at the world.

Since then, he'd felt at peace—at peace with his parents, with his friends, and especially with himself. Instead of seeing what was wrong with his life—his parents' divorce, his sister's rebellion, and everything about himself—he now saw how blessed he was. God had given him two parents who loved him and a sister who was slowly coming around.

That's what Terry had done for him. More than anything else—more than friendship and more than laughter—he'd introduced Dan to Jesus. It was a debt Dan couldn't repay. But now what? Now Terry was gone, and Dan was left wondering how something so terrible could happen to someone so good.

 **TRUTH UNPLUGGED:**

Death is not the end; it is the beginning of spending eternity with Christ once you've finished all that God has asked you to do on Earth.

"Dan, are you okay?" Dan turned to find Terry's mother standing at the door.

"Yeah, I just needed to get away," Dan said quietly. "I hope it's okay that I'm in here."

Terry's mother gave him a sad smile. "Of course. You know, sometimes I come in here and sit too. Somehow just being surrounded by his things makes me feel better."

Dan nodded.

"I still can't believe it, you know. I replay that morning over and over in my mind, trying to figure out what I could have done differently. I could have forbidden him to go swimming alone, but he was such a strong swimmer. I didn't even think about it." Tears welled up in her eyes. "I just miss him so much. Sometimes I don't know if I can make it through another day."

Dan choked, feeling tears flood his eyes. Then walking toward his best friend's mother, Dan grasped her hand. After a few minutes, they dried their eyes and left to rejoin the other guests.

As Dan walked into the living room, he saw a handful of Terry's friends from the youth group. They huddled together in a corner talking and crying. Dan joined them. They told stories about Terry. Some were funny; others were serious. The talked about missions trips to Mexico where Terry had given away all of his things to the poor people he'd met there. Then they told the story about the car-wash fundraiser where Terry had doused the pastor with the hose, thus starting an all-out water war. On and on the stories went. In each of them, Terry's personality and his love for people and Jesus came through. Again, Dan wondered how he would go on without his best friend.

Feeling like he needed some space, Dan left to go home. He just wanted to be alone to think and pray. He knew it would be awhile before he would come to terms with Terry's death. And although he didn't understand why it had happened, he knew God was the only One who would get him through it intact.

When he arrived home, his mother met him at the door. Though his mother had attended the funeral, she'd only stayed a few minutes at Terry's house. Dan knew Terry's death was hard on his mother, too, because she kept hugging him and staring at him, as if to make sure he was still there.

"Dan, you got something in the mail today," his mother said slowly.

"Okay, what is it?" Dan asked. Honestly, he couldn't have cared less. He was tired and irritable and just wanted to be left alone.

Slowly his mother handed him a postcard. Dan took it and looked at the picture on the front. Chills raced down his spine. It was a beautiful picture of the Florida coast—sandy, white beaches and aqua-colored water. Turning it over, he immediately recognized Terry's handwriting. The words blurred as tears came to his eyes and he realized it had been mailed the day before Terry died. It said:

D-

You can't imagine how incredible it is here. Pictures and stories just don't do it justice. You have to see it to believe it. See ya soon.

Keep praying!
Terry

Holding the postcard, Dan wept. Though he knew he missed his friend—and always would—he took comfort in the fact that Terry was in a better place with Jesus. Though it was hard to imagine not seeing him again in this world, Dan knew they *would* see each other again. And when they did, they'd have a lot of catching up to do!

TRUTH LINK:

Dear Lord, help me to keep my eyes on You—even in the midst of losing someone. Remind me that this world is not the end, but only the beginning of spending eternity with You. Give me the strength to face my loss without getting overwhelmed by despair. You know how much I miss this person. I know it's important for me to fulfill the purpose and plans You have for my life, so please help me to do that. Amen.

POWER UP:

Have you recently lost someone you love—a grandparent, a parent, a friend? It's a difficult thing to face. You may feel deep sorrow, shock, or anger. Remember that death is not the end. Don't let your pain turn into hopelessness. If your loved one knew Jesus as his or her Savior, then that person is in Heaven with Him now. And better yet, you'll see that special person again.

Don't get too impatient to see your loved one before the appointed time, however. Instead live your life the way Jesus wants you to live it, following Him every day. As you do, He'll give you the peace, comfort, strength, and wisdom to face each day and live your life to the fullest.

THE DRIVING DILEMMA

Patience

DOWNLOAD:

We do not want you to become lazy, but to imitate those who through faith and patience inherit what has been promised.

Hebrews 6:12 NIV

"Watch out!" Trent's father yelled from the passenger side of the car. "You have to look both ways before you pull out into traffic."

"Dad, I'm trying," Trent answered. "You're making me nervous."

"Well, pay attention to where you're going!"

"Quit yelling at me," Trent replied hotly.

"That's it," his father said with finality. "We're going home."

Walking in the garage door, Trent fell into a chair at the dinner table. His father retreated into the living room and turned on the television. Turning to his mother who stood cutting up vegetables for dinner, Trent complained, "Mom, I can't take it. Dad freaks out every time I drive with him. He totally overreacts. If there's a car within a mile of me, he's sure I'm going to hit it."

His mother smiled. "Honey, you have to be patient with him. Trust me; teaching your teenage son how to drive is a big deal."

"Patience with *him?*" Trent asked in shock. "What about patience with *me?* How am I supposed to learn how to drive when he's yelling at me?" Then staring sadly down at the paper napkin he had shredded to bits, he asked, "Why can't you teach me?"

"Trent, I know this isn't easy. But your dad really wants to be the one to teach you how to drive and to take you for your driving test. It's important to him. Just give him some time. As your driving improves, he'll relax more in the car. I promise; it'll work out."

Trent wasn't so sure. Rising from the table, he went to wash his hands for dinner. Why was his dad so tense about his driving? Sure, his dad sometimes got angry with him about other things, but usually he was pretty cool. This was one of the few things that seemed to push him over the edge.

Over dinner, Trent sat quietly. He noticed that his father was pretty quiet too. Trying to compensate for the silence, Trent's mother and little sister chatted back and forth.

His sister was noisily rambling on and on about her tennis lessons. Playing tennis was a family tradition. Trent had taken lessons when he was younger, and now it was Bethany's turn. "Trent, can you take me to the park tomorrow and help me with my serve?" Bethany asked excitedly. "I think I've almost got it, but I want you to watch me to make sure I'm doing it right."

Trent shrugged. He'd been to the park for the past three weekends showing Bethany how to serve and working with her on her backhand. It wasn't that Trent minded, but sometimes he felt like Bethany didn't listen when he tried to give her pointers. When Trent showed her a new move or tried to improve her technique, it seemed to take forever for Bethany to catch on.

"I guess," Trent said. "I just don't want to go out there and waste my time. It shouldn't take forever for you to pick up each drill."

Bethany frowned down at her plate. "I do the best I can, ya know. It's not easy."

Trent didn't respond. He noticed his mother watching him with a curious expression on her face, but he couldn't dwell on it. He had other things on his mind. How was he going to learn how to drive and be ready to take his driver's test in three months? Turning to his father, he asked, "Dad, when can we practice driving again?"

His father stopped eating and looked from Trent to his mother before saying, "I don't know. Later."

"But how am I supposed to be ready for my driving test?" Trent protested. He knew his father would probably get irritated, but he couldn't help it. He didn't want to be the *only* sixteen-year-old in school without his driver's license. He had plans. He wanted to drive his mother's car to school events and after-school band practice. If he didn't practice, he'd never be ready.

"Trent," his dad said in a tone that warned him to back off, "I said later."

Trent looked at him and then back at his mother before setting his fork on the edge of his plate. "Fine," he said. "May I be excused? I'd like to go to my room."

After being excused, he went up to his room, sat on his bed, and sulked. His dad was being so unfair. He wasn't a bad driver, surely no worse than other kids his age. He just needed to practice. Why was his dad being so stubborn? And why was his dad so impatient with him whenever they did practice? *If he would just relax,* Trent reasoned, *I'd learn, and he wouldn't drive himself to a coronary.*

Tap, tap, tap.

He heard a soft knock at his door. "Come in," he said.

Carefully, his mother slipped into the room. "How are you doing? You didn't eat much at dinner." Trent mumbled that he wasn't hungry, and his mother continued, "You know, your dad *is* going to teach you to drive. He just needs a little more time."

"Mom, we've been out twice now, and we've barely made it around the block. He gets so tense that he makes me tense. Now, he doesn't even want to take me. How am I supposed to learn?"

His mother nodded. "You're right. He needs to have more patience with you. He can't expect you to be a professional driver the first few times you get behind the wheel."

"Exactly," Trent spit out.

His mother continued nodding. "I know you're doing your best. You just need practice."

TRUTH UNPLUGGED:

Patience is an attribute you can develop through prayer and careful observation of others.

Trent nodded, although he had a strange suspicion that he was being set up for something.

"You just need someone to work with you and help you become better, like a coach," she said empathetically.

Suddenly, Trent saw where this was going. "You're comparing this to me teaching Bethany how to play tennis? Mom, it's not the same thing."

His mother didn't say anything. She just returned Trent's gaze.

"Mom, it's not," Trent persisted. "I help Bethany all the time. She just doesn't get it. I have worked with her and worked with her. It's frustrating."

Again, his mother didn't answer. Instead, she just smiled and nodded with a humorous glint in her eye. Trent could feel his face turning red. He'd treated Bethany exactly the same way his dad had been treating him. He'd gotten frustrated and short-tempered and made Bethany feel like a failure.

"Fine," he finally said. "I'll help Bethany with her tennis. I'll be more patient, and I won't make her feel like a loser just because it takes her awhile to catch on."

His mother continued smiling. "That would be really nice."

"And I'll try to give Dad a break about taking me driving. I'll try to remember that he's doing the best he can," he added.

His mother walked over to his bed and sat down. Then with a hug, she said, "You're a pretty great kid, ya know that? I'm really proud of you."

Trent smiled and hugged her back. "You're my mom. You have to say that." But Trent had to admit, it was a pretty nice thing to hear.

TRUTH LINK:

Dear Lord, help me to be patient with others so I don't get irritated when they don't do something right or when things don't go my way. Instead give me the endurance to handle things joyfully and honorably, as You would have me handle them. Amen.

POWER UP:

You know what it's like to have someone lose patience with you, but do you find yourself getting easily frustrated with people or situations? Do you sometimes think, **I just don't have the patience to deal with this?**

Well, patience is something you can develop. You can become more tolerant with family, friends, strangers, and even situations so that when things don't happen the way you expect or in the time frame you anticipate, you can have the grace to handle it. If you want more patience in your life, ask God to help you develop it. Then look for people in your life and in the Bible who have great patience. Learn from them and be aware of your emotions when you're in a tense situation. When you get the urge to become frustrated, take a deep breath and make the choice to remain calm. Count to ten if you have to. As you practice, you will become a patient person.

WORTHLESS

Suicide

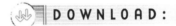

DOWNLOAD:

"This is how much God loved the world: He gave his Son, his one
and only Son. And this is why: so that no one need be destroyed;
by believing in him, anyone can have a whole and lasting life."

John 3:16

Ben sat on his bedroom floor, holding the small handgun. It
was heavier than he had thought it would be. And the longer he
held it, the heavier it became. Would he have the nerve to follow
through with his plan? But then again, what was the alternative?
Continue with life the way it's been? No, that isn't an option, he
thought, holding back angry tears.

He'd heard his parents argue about him. "Well, you're never
around," his mother had thrown at his father. "You're supposed to
take him every other weekend, but you cancel as often as you
take him. I need time off too, ya know."

"What? So you can be with the latest boyfriend you drag home? Give me a break," his father had shot back. "You're his mother for God's sake. You can't expect me to make up for the messes you cause." Back and forth they went.

They'd been divorced for years. The only time they even spoke was when Ben had made a mistake or the child support was late. Whenever it came to him and his problems, they reveled at pointing the finger at each other. Each said the other was to blame.

Ben closed his eyes, thinking how nice it would be not having to hear them argue anymore. He could be free. He wouldn't have to put up with any more of his mother's latest flings hanging around the house trying to buddy up to him. And he wouldn't be forced to sit through another drilling from his father about what he wanted to do with his life. His father often preached to Ben that he needed to be decisive and work hard instead of wasting time on frivolous, teenage things. Ben had always suspected that the pep talks had come from his dad counting the days until Ben turned eighteen, so he could stop sending monthly child support.

Not that he blamed them. He had to admit that he was nothing to be proud of. He had tried to be the perfect son, but he couldn't help himself. He wasn't good-looking. He wasn't smart. He wasn't a comedian. He didn't have many friends. "Who could care about someone like me?" he said out loud to the empty room.

Looking around his room, he began to prepare. He didn't want there to be a lot for his mother to clean up, so he decided to do it on the bed so his mother could just throw out the bedding. She wouldn't have to replace any carpet or repaint any walls. He'd be careful.

Would they miss me, he wondered, *even a little bit?*

Maybe his dad would miss a day of work for his funeral. Maybe he'd even turn off his cell phone, but at least he wouldn't have to send any more child support.

And what about his mother? Would she drag the latest loser to Ben's funeral? *I hope not,* Ben thought.

Then he stopped. What about Grandma Lil? He hadn't thought about her. Grandma Lil would miss him—a lot. Sitting Indian-style on the floor, he thought about the only person who made him feel loved, Grandma Lil.

She was everything a grandmother should be: warm, loving, strong, and smart. Ben loved visiting Grandma Lil on her farm. She was in her sixties, but she still kept a small farm out in the country with chickens and a garden and even an old cow that she milked every day. When he was there, he always felt useful and safe. He helped his grand-mother tend the garden and collect the eggs from the chickens and even milk the cow. And when they sat down to a garden-fresh, made-from-scratch meal, they always held hands and said grace.

 **TRUTH UNPLUGGED:**

Suicide is never an answer to the hopelessness you feel. God has wonderful plans for your life, so don't give up.

Normally, Ben didn't go to church. It just wasn't something his parents had ever done, but when he was at Grandma Lil's, he couldn't imagine not going. Sitting in the small, old church house, he felt just as cared for as he did sitting in Grandma Lil's kitchen.

Ben loved those visits. They were few and far between, though. It wasn't that his grandmother lived that far away, but Ben's parents were usually too busy to take him, and Grandma Lil didn't like driving in the city. She said it made her too nervous.

Wondering what he should do, Ben decided that he should at least call Grandma Lil one more time, kind of a last good-bye. Walking over to the phone that sat beside his bed, Ben dialed her number.

"Ben," his grandmother cried after Ben identified himself. "How's my best grandson?"

"Fine, Grandma. I just wanted to call and say hi."

"You know, it's the strangest thing," his grandmother began, her voice taking on a serious note. "You've been on my mind all day. I've been praying, asking God to take care of my grandboy. Are you sure you're okay?"

Ben felt a lump rise in his throat. "Sure, Grandma, I'm okay," he choked out.

His grandmother was quiet for a moment before answering, "Well, I've been thinking it's time for a visit. When can you come?"

"I don't know. I'll have to talk to Mom and see when she can bring me."

"Phooey. I'll come get you myself. When can you come?" his grandmother responded with determination.

"But, Grandma, you don't like driving in the city," Ben said weakly.

"Don't you worry about that. I'll get one of my girlfriends to drive me to get you, and you and I will make a day of it." As Ben listened, the tears that he had held back began to trickle down his face, and try as he might, sobs got caught in his throat. "Oh, Ben," his grandmother responded to his crying. "God sees you. He let me know that you needed your grandma. I love you so much. You have no idea how special you are."

Ben could hear the emotion in his grandmother's voice, and he felt her love all the way through the phone line. "Now," his grandmother continued, "I want you to get that little Bible I gave you last Christmas." Ben slowly rose to retrieve the little Bible from his bookshelf. "Open it up to the table of contents and find the Book of John in the New Testament. Now, I want you to read the whole Book of John. You'll see that Jesus loves you and that He died for you. You are not alone. He's right there with you." Ben promised to read it. Then his grandmother added, "I'll call your mother at work right now and make arrangements to pick you up tomorrow, so you be ready."

After Ben hung up the phone, he felt more hopeful than he'd felt in a long, long time. Opening the Bible, he began to read. As the pages unfolded, Ben felt a peace come over him that he hadn't ever sensed before. After finishing the Book of John, he went on to the next book, Acts, eager to find out the rest of the story.

Slowly, he realized that he wasn't so worthless after all. If what he read was true, the God of the universe seemed to think he was valuable and worthwhile. Closing his eyes, Ben silently began to talk to God about all the feelings he'd hidden from everyone else for so long. Though he didn't hear an audible response, he knew, without a doubt, that God was listening and answering him. He knew God loved him enough to think that what he had to say was pretty important.

TRUTH LINK:

Dear Lord, I'm at the end of my rope. I'm so scared and miserable that I'm desperate to stop the pain any way I can—even if it means ending my life. I've heard people say that things will get better, but I don't know if I can hold on. Please help me. Show me who I can turn to or what I can do to make the pain stop. Amen.

POWER UP:

Have you ever been tempted to end your life? That is not God's solution for your situation. He loves you, and He wants to help you. Ask Him to direct you to someone you can trust—a family member, a friend, a pastor, or a counselor. Don't try to face this alone. And don't entertain thoughts of ending your life. You are more valuable and precious than words could ever describe, and God has a plan for your life that is far better than the hopelessness you feel right now.

THE EASY WAY OUT

Lying

DOWNLOAD:

What this adds up to, then, is this: no more lies, no more pretense. Tell your neighbor the truth. In Christ's body we're all connected to each other, after all. When you lie to others, you end up lying to yourself. Ephesians 4:25

Evan called the yearbook meeting to order. "We have a lot to discuss this week, so let's get started," he began. "First, we have to come up with a theme for the yearbook. Anyone have any ideas?"

It was Evan's first year as yearbook editor. After working on it for the past two years, he finally had the chance to take charge. He was so excited to meet with the rest of the yearbook team and to hash out the details. Bantering ideas back and forth, the team grew passionate. Several wanted to base the theme on a popular song. Others wanted to base it on current events, and one or two threw out ideas that were completely off the wall.

Evan loved the creative process, but the meeting also helped him get an idea of his team's strengths. Kathy, another yearbook veteran, was very creative. Then Sam and Mike were great photographers—very visual. Debra loved to write, so her ideas were geared toward puns and plays on words. Then there was the newbie—a freshman named Jeri. Jeri had worked on her junior high yearbook, so she had some experience, but Evan still thought she was too new to the whole process. She had a lot to learn.

After the meeting, Jeri approached him. "Evan, I wanted to run an idea past you. My uncle is a photographer in town, and he's willing to do some really different shots for the seniors this year. He lives on a farm with a lake, and he can do some great outdoors shots." Then handing Evan a stack of photos, she added, "He took these of me last year. He's really good."

Evan flipped through the photos. They were good—really different from the typical senior photos. They looked more like photos out of a professional magazine. He'd incorporated the lake as a background and had also taken beautiful shots of Jeri among some wildflowers. "These *are* good," he admitted. "But we already use Bryson Photography. We have for years."

"Yeah, I know, but maybe we could give the students a choice. My uncle did say he'd give the students a great deal."

"Okay, let me talk to Mrs. Glenn, our sponsor, about it," Evan said, handing the photos back to her.

Within a few weeks, the yearbook was in full swing. The staff began to lay out several ideas for spreads. They'd come up with the theme and started getting the clubs involved in planning their pages. They had also received orders for advertisements. Evan started to feel the pressure of bringing everything together on time and under budget.

One day, Jeri came up to him and asked, "Hey Evan, have you talked to Mrs. Glenn yet about using my uncle?"

Evan stopped. It had completely slipped his mind. "No, I haven't talked to her about it yet. I'll talk to her this week. Sorry, I gotta go." He turned and rushed down the hall. Evan didn't mean to blow Jeri off, but he was way too busy to think about Jeri's photographer uncle.

Over the next few weeks, Jeri asked Evan several times about using her uncle. Each time, Evan dodged the question. It wasn't that he had anything against Jeri or her uncle, but Evan had a lot on his mind, and Jeri's pushiness was wearing a little thin. After all, this was her first year on the yearbook. Why couldn't she just let it go? They already had a photographer. Sticking with the regular photographer would simplify things. And right now Evan needed things simple.

At one of their weekly meetings, Jeri again asked if he had talked to Mrs. Glenn. Exasperated, Evan responded emphatically, "Yes, I have. We're sticking with Bryson Photography. Let's move on."

Jeri looked at him in disbelief, because her uncle's work was so obviously superior, disappointed that the decision had been made without even discussing it with the rest of the yearbook team.

A couple of days later, Evan was working late in the yearbook room when Jeri entered. "I need to talk to you," Jeri said flatly.

Evan looked up, "Okay. What's up?" He could tell she was angry.

"Why'd you lie to me?" Jeri asked hotly with her hands on her hips. "You said you'd talked to Mrs. Glenn about using my uncle as a photographer, but you never did. I know because I talked to her about it today, and she thinks it's a great idea."

"You went behind my back?" Evan asked in surprise.

"Well, I didn't like your answer. There was no reason for it. Bryson Photography is lame. The students complain about them every year, so why not give them a choice?"

"How do you know the students complain every year? You're a *freshman*," Evan shot back.

"Oh, I get it. My opinion doesn't count because I'm just a lowly freshman. Well, that's stupid, Mr. Yearbook Editor. I'm on this team too," Jeri said angrily. "And just for the record, it doesn't take a brain surgeon to know Bryson Photography is lame. I have two older brothers. They went to Bryson Photography for their yearbook photos and my uncle for the ones they gave away. Everyone loved the ones my uncle did."

"I really don't care if your uncle is the best photographer in the world. It's easier to use one photographer. We're using Bryson," Evan said with finality.

 TRUTH UNPLUGGED:

Lying destroys relationships. It drives a wedge between the person who lies and those who hear and believe the lie.

"Really? Well, Mrs. Glenn will be calling you about that and about the fact that you lied about talking it over with her," Jeri said crossing her arms. "And you can bet I'll be showing my uncle's photos to the rest of the yearbook team."

"I'm the editor. I've decided to use Bryson, and that's that."

"Anyone who'd rather lie than think about what's best for the students isn't fit to be editor," Jeri said, storming out of the room.

Evan was furious. He hadn't *meant* to lie about meeting with Mrs. Glenn. He'd just gotten tired of Jeri asking him about it, and he'd been too busy to be bothered. And Jeri was right. Evan hadn't given her credit for coming up with a good idea, and it was because she was a freshman. And instead of following through on what he said he'd do, he'd allowed himself to take the easy way out—he lied. Now he was going to have to face Mrs. Glenn.

The following day, Mrs. Glenn confronted him about lying to Jeri and not taking the time to consider Jeri's idea. She talked to him about good leadership and telling the truth—even in difficult or stressful situations. Mrs. Glenn told him that it was up to him to work this mess out since he'd caused it. Mrs. Glenn also warned that if he wasn't up for the challenge of being yearbook editor, maybe he should resign.

Evan promised that wasn't the case.

Walking into the yearbook meeting the following day, Evan stood at the front. He could feel the tension around the table. Jeri had already told people about her fight with Evan and Evan's lie. She'd also shown her uncle's pictures to them. The senior class was buzzing with excitement at the chance to have their pictures taken by him.

Nervous, Evan began to speak, "I'm sure everyone has already heard about the addition of the new senior-class photographer. The seniors will have the choice to use Jeri's uncle for their senior pictures." Then stopping to take a breath he continued, "I also need to apologize to Jeri for not being honest with her last week. I said that I'd talked to Mrs. Glenn about using her uncle when in fact, I hadn't. I just got busy with everything, and it slipped my mind. Then when she put me on the spot, I said I had. I'm really sorry."

As the meeting continued, the tension eased. Evan made a point of listening to everyone's ideas around the table. He was surprised to realize that Jeri had several good ones. Afterwards, Evan pulled Jeri aside to apologize again. She accepted his apology, though Evan knew it would be awhile before she forgot the incident.

There's a lot more to being yearbook editor than getting my own way, he thought as he watched Jeri leave. *In fact, it would be a lot less stressful if I'd take advantage of suggestions from the team.*

TRUTH LINK:

Dear Lord, please forgive me for saying anything less than the absolute truth. Even when it seems easier to lie, help me to be honest. Amen.

POWER UP:

Have you ever been in a situation where it seemed easier to lie, or fib, than tell the absolute, 100 percent truth? Everyone has. Though lying may seem like the easiest answer at the time, it **CAN** come back to haunt you.

As someone lies, it becomes easier the next time and the next time after that. Then one day, the truth comes out, and the lie is exposed. After that, it takes a lot of time and energy to rebuild the trust of others. When it comes down to it—it's just not worth it. Though the truth may be difficult in the short run, it will save your relationships and self-respect in the long run.

MAN VS. MACHINE

Materialism

DOWNLOAD:

A life devoted to things is a dead life, a stump; a God-shaped life is a flourishing tree. Proverbs 11:28

Brad couldn't believe the day was finally here. At sixteen years old, he was about to buy his very own car, and not just any car—a 1968 Camaro. It just didn't get any better than that.

He'd saved for years. In fact, he started saving for this car at ten years old. He'd done whatever he could to make money after school, on weekends, and during summer vacations—pulled weeds, mowed yards, walked dogs, washed cars, and anything else his parents and neighbors allowed him to do.

Every so often, he'd tell his dad, "I am going to be so *cool* when I get this car! My friends are going to die when they see it."

His dad usually smiled and responded with something like, "The car doesn't make the man, son."

In response, Brad would smile and nod, but inside he disagreed. Being the envy of all the other kids at school was a big deal. What could be better? Of course, if he got the car and the girl, it *would* be better.

Brad dreamed about asking Lana Murphy out. She was the prettiest and most popular girl in school. Up until now, Brad hadn't had the nerve to do it, but with the coolest car in school, he figured he could move up the popularity ranks and be in a good place to ask Lana for a date.

He knew Shellie wouldn't be thrilled about him dating Lana. Shellie and Brad had been friends for years. She lived down the street. Brad knew she liked him; she'd made it pretty obvious. She had invited him to outings with friends and always came to his baseball games. Last year, she'd even thrown him a surprise birthday party. Sometimes Brad thought about Shellie as more than a friend, but as much as he liked her, he couldn't get Lana out of his mind. Sure, Shellie was pretty and fun, but Lana was beautiful and super popular. Every guy in school wanted to go out with her.

If I ask Lana out, Shellie will be hurt, he thought. *But I have to do it.* He couldn't help himself; he had to try.

Behind the wheel of his new car, Brad felt like a king. He drove home with the windows down, enjoying the air whipping through his hair. After years of planning, he'd done it. It was all his.

He had to show it off. First, he wanted to show it to Shellie. More than anyone, she knew how much he'd worked for it. As he pulled into her driveway and honked, she raced out her front door to meet him. "Brad, congratulations! It's gorgeous!" She jumped into the passenger side, and together, they took a drive around town. They drove down the city strip where all of their friends hung out and toured the local burger joint, so Brad could show off his car to some of the guys from his baseball team. He was in heaven. Just as he had imagined, he was the envy of all his friends.

On Monday, he drove into the school parking lot and took care to park his car away from any large trucks or cars with big doors that might damage it. He'd worked too hard to get this car to let anyone dent the doors.

Before school, Brad spotted Lana standing with a large group of her friends. Taking a deep breath, he walked up to the group and said, "Hey Lana, how's it going?"

Turning to face him, she smiled. "Oh hey, Brad. I'm fine. How are you? I heard you got a new car. Congratulations."

"Yeah, it's pretty cool. I've been saving for a long time."

Lana smiled in response.

Wow! Is she pretty, Brad thought as he said good-bye and walked to his homeroom class. *I have got to ask her out!*

After school, Brad walked out to the parking lot and saw Lana on her way to her car. Taking the plunge, he walked up and asked her to a movie on Friday night. When she accepted, he thought he'd pass out from excitement. Playing it cool, he replied, "Cool. I'll pick you up at six." After they'd exchanged phone numbers and directions to her house, he walked shakily back to his car and drove home. It wasn't until he was halfway home that he allowed himself to shout, "Oh yeah!" into the air.

It quickly got around school that he'd asked Lana out on a date. Though he hated it, he intentionally avoided Shellie. He knew she'd hear about the date sooner or later, and he didn't want to see her reaction. He could probably handle an outright confrontation; it was the heavy silence or dancing around the subject that he couldn't handle. It was better to avoid the situation, but even that was hard. He missed her.

On Friday night, Brad dressed for his date. He had made sure his car was in perfect condition—hand-waxed the outside and cleaned the inside with Armorall. When he opened the door for

Lana, he saw a distasteful look cross her face. "What's wrong?" he asked.

"Oh nothing," she said with some surprise. "I just thought you got a *new* car. I didn't realize it was old."

Brad looked at her with obvious shock. "This is a classic."

"Uh-huh," she said with a forced smile.

At that point, Brad knew the date was pretty much over. The evening proved him right. It quickly went downhill from there. Brad discovered that he and Lana had about as much in common as a tire and a spark plug. They were both people, but beyond that—nothing.

The next day Brad went to Shellie's. When she came to the door, she looked at him with surprise and a flicker of irritation. "So how was your date?" she asked quickly with an edge.

TRUTH UNPLUGGED:

Material things don't determine your value.

"Not good," he said flatly.

She smiled and nodded in response as though she wasn't a bit surprised. "I could have told you that Lana wasn't the girl you thought she was. Beyond being pretty, there's not much else there." Brad laughed and agreed.

Then Shellie invited him in to play a video game. As they played, Brad realized that Shellie had been his friend a long time before he got the car, and while she was happy that he'd realized his dream, she wasn't swayed to be his friend because of it.

I guess that's what real friends are for, he thought. *Hmm—I wonder if Shellie would like to see a movie next Friday night?*

TRUTH LINK:

Dear Lord, thank You for reminding me that things don't determine my value. You love me for who I am in You, and You've placed people in my life who love me for who You've made me. Please help me to remember that. Keep me from falling into the trap of thinking that I have to look a certain way or have certain things to be valuable. Amen.

POWER UP:

Everywhere, people—the news, Hollywood, magazines, friends, even family—tell you how to look, how to dress, and what to own. If you're not careful, you can begin to believe that these things dictate the kind of person you are. You can begin to think that if you don't have the perfect clothes or just the right car or the ideal house, then you're nobody.

But that's not true. God is interested in who you are as a person, not the material things around you. It isn't wrong to have nice things, but it is wrong to define yourself by them. The next time you think you need to have some **THING** to make you worthwhile, remember that one day, not too far in the future, that **THING's** popularity will be replaced by something newer. Whereas, the values God has put in you—love, joy, peace, kindness, etc.—will last forever.

WHAT ABOUT THEM?

Racism

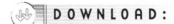 **DOWNLOAD:**

"Let me give you a new command: Love one another. In the same way I loved you, you love one another. This is how everyone will recognize that you are my disciples—when they see the love you have for each other." John 13:34-35

Shawn walked into work at the DooWop Diner at 4:45 P.M. for the evening shift. It was going to be a long night. He had stayed up to finish a project for Spanish class the night before, so he'd only gotten a few hours of sleep. After going to school all day, here he was—ready to put in five solid hours on his feet.

He really liked his job at the diner. Harry, his boss, was nice, and the atmosphere was fun. The other waiters and waitresses made it lively and action-packed between the constant jokes and the corny birthday song they had to sing whenever a customer had a birthday. It all kept him laughing, that was for sure.

As Shawn strapped on his apron, he noticed a new guy standing with Harry. The guy was obviously going through orientation. The thing that Shawn noticed right away was that the guy was Middle Eastern. He looked like the Arab faces that Shawn had seen all over the news since 9/11. Shawn hadn't ever known a Middle Easterner, but since 9/11, it didn't matter; he didn't trust any of them.

Grabbing his pen and order pad, he walked to the front to relieve another waiter. As he walked by Harry and the new guy, Harry called to him. "Shawn, this is Amad. Tonight is his first night."

Shawn eyed him suspiciously and gave him a consolatory smile. "Hi," he said simply. The guy smiled back with a warm and slightly nervous smile.

"Shawn has been here for six months," Harry said. "He's a good one to ask about the way things are done around here." Shawn smiled at Harry. Then with a parting glance toward Amad, he walked away. He wasn't excited about being Amad's "go to" person. He would have preferred that Harry ask someone else, but he guessed he didn't have much choice now.

The night passed uneventfully. Shawn only talked to Amad when it was absolutely necessary. He answered his questions and showed him where things were located in the diner. He helped him with procedures and introduced him to a few of the wait staff that Amad hadn't met yet. Their conversations were short and to the point.

Shawn just didn't trust him.

Later that week, when a Middle Eastern family walked in the front door of the diner, Shawn hesitated. They looked like any normal family, but in light of past events, Shawn wasn't sure he could trust them. Rather than spending the whole night feeling uncomfortable, he chose to ignore them. Before long, Amad sat them in his area.

They'll probably be more comfortable with Amad anyway, Shawn told himself. But then he thought, *I hope more of them don't start showing up.*

A few days later, Shawn walked into the kitchen and noticed Amad standing in the corner with his hands on his hips and his back rigid, like he was upset. Though Shawn didn't want to get involved, his compassion won out. "Are you alright?" he asked.

Amad jerked when he heard Shawn's voice and took a deep breath. "Yeah, sure. I'm fine." He straightened his apron. "I just had a rude customer."

Shawn nodded. "That happens sometimes," he said sympathetically.

"Yeah, well, these people said they refused to be waited on by an Iraqi," he said in disgust. "It's so stupid. I'm not even of Iraqi descent. I was born in the U.S. like everyone else. I'm certainly no terrorist."

TRUTH UNPLUGGED:

Racism holds you back from experiencing the value God has placed in people.

Shawn didn't respond; instead he just stood listening.

"You know, my parents came to this country to live in freedom, just like everyone else. They just got here a little late." Amad began picking up steam as he continued. "I can't help it if I look like those crazy people from 9/11."

Shawn began to feel uncomfortable. He had to admit he had thought the same thing as the people who had refused to allow Amad to wait on them. "You know, I kinda judged you because of the way you look too," Shawn admitted quietly.

Amad looked up and smiled. "I know. I could feel it. You know, I never used to experience much prejudice before 9/11. I mean, sure it happened every once in a while, but in general, people were nice to my family and me. But all of that has changed. Now, people who are normally really nice look at us like we're a bunch of terrorists." Then laughing he added, "I was actually surprised that Harry hired me. The only thing I can figure is that he's sympathetic because he's African-American."

Shawn smiled. "He's a really fair man, even more so than I am, I guess."

"Don't beat yourself up," Amad said. "It was a little weird for me after 9/11, too, just wondering who to trust. Those people were just crazy, I guess."

"Were they typical of the Islamic religion?" Shawn asked.

Amad shrugged. "I don't know. I'm a Christian. That's another reason my parents left their country. Christians were being persecuted for their religious beliefs."

"I'm sorry," Shawn said, shaking his head and laughing. "I totally misjudged you, man. Here I thought you were from the Middle East and that you were Islamic and possibly a terrorist. Now I find out that you're as American as I am. We're both Christians, and neither of us understand why those people did what they did on 9/11."

After accepting Shawn's apology, the two of them went back to work. As Shawn got to know Amad, he discovered that they had a lot in common. They both felt strongly about their faith. They both loved working at the diner, and they were both in the same grade in school. He also discovered that Amad had the funniest sense of humor. In time, they became great friends.

Shawn promised himself that in the future, whenever he met a person of Middle Eastern descent, he would remember Amad. He would try to get to know the person instead of letting fear and suspicion cloud his judgment. And though the media was constantly reminding viewers that anyone of Arab descent could be a terrorist in hiding, he decided the old adage "Don't judge a book by its cover" was a good way to live.

TRUTH LINK:

Dear Lord, I want to love people the way You do—unconditionally, regardless of their race. I pray that You'll take any racist thoughts out of my heart and mind so I can be free to be an example of Christ in everything I do. Amen.

 POWER UP:

Have you ever found yourself judging people based on the color of their skin or their ethnic origin? Maybe you've heard that a group of people is lazy or stingy. Maybe you've heard that they could be dangerous or take advantage of you, and because of that, you have viewed them with suspicion or automatically disliked them.

Well, if so, watch out; you've just crossed over into racism. Racism isn't always as blatant as burning crosses in someone's front yard or flagrant hateful speech; it's also about automatically viewing someone with suspicion and reserve just because they're different.

If you have those feelings and fears, take them to God. He wants to free you to love people and view people the way He does. He wants and needs you to be an example of how to treat others. Remember, you are His hands and His feet in this world.

NUDGES

Holy Spirit

DOWNLOAD:

"My sheep listen to my voice; I know them, and they follow me." John 10:27 NIV

"Brian, I'm ready to play now!" Zach said, bursting into Brian's bedroom.

Brian rolled his eyes. "Zach, I don't have time right now. I gotta go."

"But yesterday you promised that you'd play Indie Speed IV with me this afternoon," Zach whined.

Brian continued putting on his sneakers, giving his eight-year-old brother a sideways glance. "Look, I can't just drop everything every time you wanna play. I have a life, too, ya know? Now, let me finish getting ready. The guys are picking me up in five minutes."

"But you promised!" Zach cried.

"Yeah, well sometimes people have to break promises," Brian threw out. Then he paused and took a deep breath of resignation. "Listen, I'll try to get home early, so we can play a few rounds on the computer before bedtime, okay?"

"Whatever. You promised yesterday that you'd play with me this afternoon, and you lied. So why should I believe you now?" And with that Zach stormed out of the room, slamming the door as he went.

Sometimes Brian wanted to strangle his little brother. Zach could be so demanding—and it had gotten worse after their parents' divorce last year. Brian knew how much Zach loved hanging out with him, but what could he do? His friends had called earlier that morning and asked him to play football in the park and then go out for pizza. How could he pass that up? So what if he had to break a silly promise to his brother? They'd have plenty of time for computer games later.

Suddenly, Brian stopped. He felt it. A nudge.

After their parents had split up, they'd started attending church every week with their mom. At first, Brian had thought it would be lame, but actually, he enjoyed it. He'd given His heart to the Lord and had met some great friends at youth group. He liked the pastor too. He couldn't count the number of times he'd been upset about his parents' divorce or something at school, and then, he'd go to youth group. It was as if the pastor spoke directly to him every time. And now, he'd started getting—well, nudges—about things around him.

At first he'd thought the "nudges" were just his imagination, or at best—his conscience going into overdrive. But then Brian's youth pastor at church talked about listening to the Holy Spirit. When he had first shown up at youth group, he thought the pastor was *a little off* when he'd start talking about God speaking to you. But now Brian had to admit that there were times when he knew he was having those nudging feelings and—they weren't his own.

Sometimes the nudges even came as thoughts. Small stuff, really. There had been the time when he'd felt like he should go straight home after school instead of going over to a friend's house. Then when he arrived home, he found his mom upset after a difficult day. Or he'd heard, "Don't go to that party." Then later he learned that a rough crowd had shown up or that alcohol had been served. He had learned to trust those quiet suggestions. He knew he hadn't hit the mark 100 percent of the time, but he was trying.

Just then, Brian heard his friend John's car horn. He grabbed his jacket, flew down the stairs, and stopped. To his right he could see Zach lying on the couch with the TV remote in his hand, flipping through channels. Zach glanced over at Brian and then back at the TV. Brian could tell he was mad. And he felt a small pang in his stomach. A nudge again.

"So, I'll see you later tonight. We'll play Indie Speed IV when I get back," Brian said, trying to smooth over the situation.

"Whatever," Zach said, never taking his eyes off the television screen.

"Okay, bye."

With that, Brian headed out the door. He ran down the front steps and jumped into the car. All the way to the park, Brian's friends laughed and joked back and forth, but Brian couldn't join the fun. He kept seeing Zach lying on the couch, disappointed, oozing with anger. And Brian couldn't quite shake the uneasiness in his stomach. "But you promised!" Brian kept hearing Zach's cry over and over again in his mind.

So what? he thought. *I can still play with Zach later. And we have all tomorrow afternoon. Why is it such a big deal?*

"But you promised!" echoed again in his mind.

As they arrived at the park and joined the football game that was already in progress, Brian's uneasiness didn't go away. Though he tried to keep his mind on the game, he couldn't shake the feeling that something was off.

"Hey, Brian, what's wrong with you? You were wide open, and that last throw was perfect. You couldn't have asked for a better pass," John remarked.

"Sorry—my head's just not in the game," Brian said.

"No kidding. What's up with you anyway? You've been quiet all day," John pointed out.

"Nothing. I just . . . well, I was kind of a jerk to my kid brother earlier. I promised him I'd play with him this afternoon, and then I came here instead. He's mad, and—I just feel bad about it. That's all."

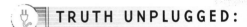

TRUTH UNPLUGGED:

You will find more peace in your life when you follow those gentle nudges.

"Sounds like you feel guilty," John pointed out.

"I don't know. Actually, it's more than that. I just feel—like I'm not where I'm supposed to be, ya know?"

"You want me to take you home?"

Brian stood there a moment watching the other guys throw the ball down the field, debating what he should do. All of a sudden, he smirked. *I think this is what the pastor calls 'feeling convicted,'* he thought. Then pausing another second, he said, "Yeah, ya know, I do need to go home. I promised Zach I'd spend the day with him, and I won't get any peace until I do what I said I'd do. Do ya mind?"

"No, man. Lemme get my keys."

"Thanks, John. I owe you."

TRUTH LINK:

Dear Lord, thank You for giving me Your Holy Spirit to guide me. Please help me recognize Your voice when I hear it, and help me listen to Your Spirit and not ignore or miss the nudges You give me.

POWER UP:

Are you someone God can count on to do what He leads you to do? Do you know when He speaks to your heart? Do you stop long enough to listen?

God speaks to us in many ways. He can speak through someone else, through His written Word, or even directly to our hearts. You sense when it's happening. Maybe He's trying to protect you from a wrong decision or dangerous situation. Or perhaps He wants to use you to help someone else. Don't miss an opportunity to follow Him in every situation. You'll be glad you did.

THE LAST LAUGH

Bullying

DOWNLOAD:

"If I, the Master and Teacher, washed your feet, you must now wash each other's feet. I've laid down a pattern for you. What I've done, you do." John 13:14-15

Lonny saw Jed Stiles sitting in the corner of the cafeteria at lunch trying to stay out of sight. Lonny laughed. *He's such an easy target,* he thought to himself. It wasn't that Lonny meant to be harsh. He just liked having a good laugh, and Jed Stiles definitely provided a good laugh.

Jed was short and puny and looked like his mother dressed him. He was terrible at anything physical, and gym class was pure torture for him. Once again, he was an easy target. Sure, he made good grades and was considered a "brain," but to Lonny, he was still just an amusing mark.

Making his way across the cafeteria, Lonny motioned to a few of his friends. Since it was common for Lonny to pick on Jed, everyone knew where he was headed. Enjoying the sport, several followed him at a distance or at least sat up a little straighter to watch the display.

Jed was in the middle of taking a drink of soda when Lonny tipped his can up even further, causing him to spill soda down his shirt. "Hey, Stiles. How's it goin?" he said in mock interest, sitting down across from Jed.

Jed's eyes darted left and right, taking in the growing crowd. "Fine," he said slowly. "What do you want?"

"Nothing. I just saw my good friend Jed sitting over here in the corner, and I wanted to say hi. So hi," Lonny said, enjoying the look on Jed's face change from surprise to panic. Then picking up a piece of white cake from Jed's plate, Lonny took a huge bite out of it.

"Why don't you just leave me alone?" Jed said with tired resignation.

Lonny laughed. "Why would I do that when you're such a good friend? Just being around you makes me happy." Wiping some of the cake's frosting onto his finger, he reached across and smeared it on Jed's face. Behind him, the crowd smirked. Jed just sat there, the blood draining from his face.

The bell rang, signaling the end of lunch. Lonny jumped to his feet with a grin on his face. "Thanks for the entertainment, Jed. See ya tomorrow." Then Lonny walked to his next class.

Up and down the halls, people laughed as Lonny walked by, congratulating him on making Jed squirm—again. Lonny loved it. He didn't mean any harm to Jed; he was just having fun. Surely, Jed had figured that out by now. Not that Lonny spent much time thinking about what Jed did or didn't think. He was too busy enjoying the limelight as the school prankster.

Later that week, Lonny took another opportunity to laugh at Jed's expense. As Jed walked down the hall on his way to class,

Lonny silently walked up behind him and kicked the bottom of one of his shoes, causing Jed to stumble and drop his books. Papers scattered everywhere. Laughter echoed down the hall as people saw Lonny standing over Jed with his arms comically thrown into the air in victory.

"Way to hustle, Stiles," he bellowed. Then shaking his head, he laughed. "You're just too easy of a target, Jed. I just can't help myself when I see you." Amused, Lonny watched as Jed gathered his papers and then quietly escaped to his next class.

The next week, Lonny again approached Jed during lunch. "Hey there, Jed, my friend," he said. "I haven't seen you in a few days. Where you been hiding?"

"I haven't been hiding," Jed said with a scowl. "I've been home sick."

"Aww," Lonny said in mock sympathy. "And here I was going to invite you to my church's carnival. We needed a clown." He watched as Jed's expression went from stunned to disgust.

"You go to church?" he asked flatly.

"Sure do. First Fellowship Church," he responded with pride.

"You're a Christian?" Jed asked in disbelief.

"Yeah, so? You have a problem with that?"

Jed shook his head and laughed a spiteful laugh. "That's the first funny thing you've ever said to me." Confused, Lonny frowned. "Let me get this straight," Jed continued. "You make my life miserable for years. You embarrass me every chance you get. You humiliate me in gym class. You make me the laughingstock of the school, so much so that I've been counting the days until I can graduate and get out of here, and now you tell me that you're a love-your-neighbor-as-yourself Christian? Give me a break."

Lonny sat speechless.

He knew he'd given Jed a hard time over the years, but he'd had no idea that he'd made Jed's life so miserable. Sure, he'd made him the butt of a few jokes along the way, but Jed knew it was just a joke, didn't he? "Hey man, I was just giving you a hard time. I didn't mean anything by all that."

Jed looked at him with pure hate in his eyes. "You didn't mean it?" he asked through clenched teeth. "You pathetic Christian. You may not have meant it, but I do mean this: I hate your guts. You make me understand why some kids resort to bringing a gun to school and getting even with bullies like you. If it wouldn't ruin my life, I would easily kill you a thousand times over. And if being a Christian means being anything like you, I'll never be one. You make me sick." Then grabbing his tray, Jed jumped up and stormed away.

Lonny continued to sit there. He'd been to church his entire life. He'd heard all the messages of loving others and being an example of Christ to the world. Until that very moment, Lonny had thought he was doing pretty well. He didn't party. He didn't fool around with girls. He didn't cuss. He didn't cheat. Nothing. But turning to watch Jed stalk away, Lonny realized that he'd failed miserably at one of the most basic elements of Christianity. And now, Jed equated Christianity with Lonny.

Ashamed, Lonny gathered his things and slowly walked to his next class. He spent the rest of the day in a depressed fog. Later, when he saw Jed walking toward him in the hall, he looked away. He couldn't face Jed or his hateful look again.

Later that week, Lonny attended his church's youth group. During the prayer time at the end of service, he went forward to pray. He prayed for forgiveness for having treated Jed so miserably for so many years, and he also asked God to show him what to do now. He kept seeing Jed's face and hearing his words: "If being a Christian means being anything like you, I'll never be one." As he continued to pray, he knew what he had to do.

The next day he found Jed sitting in the corner of the cafeteria as usual. He walked up to Jed's table and asked if he could sit down. Jed looked around as if waiting for the embarrassment to begin. "I need to talk to you," Lonny said quietly.

Jed shrugged, indicating that it was okay for Lonny to have a seat.

"I owe you an apology. In fact, I probably owe you a thousand apologies. I'm really sorry that I've been such a jerk to you."

Jed watched him with doubt written all over his face. "Why are you apologizing now? You've been a jerk for years."

"I just never thought about it from your perspective," Lonny stammered. "It was all just fun and games to me. I never thought about how my teasing must make you feel. The other day when you told me what you thought of me, it kind of hit me. I've been a real jerk and a *really* bad Christian. I am so sorry."

 TRUTH UNPLUGGED:

Your actions can either draw people to Jesus or push them away. Bullying—either being a physical threat or making someone the object of ridicule—will never bring someone to Jesus; it will only drive them away.

"So are you gonna stop?" Jed asked.

"Yeah, I'm gonna stop. I won't pick on you anymore," Lonny promised. He watched as Jed's face relaxed, as if a hundred-pound weight had been removed.

Lonny excused himself and walked away. He knew that he and Jed weren't going to suddenly become friends, but he hoped that in time, they could be. Maybe Jed would realize that being a Christian really wasn't a horrible thing.

Shaking his head as he walked, Lonny realized that all of those lectures he'd heard about being an example were right. He was an example for Christ—either a positive one or a negative one. In the future, he promised to be a positive one, bringing people to Christ instead of driving them away.

TRUTH LINK:

Dear Lord, help me to be an example of Jesus' love to the world. I don't want to push people away from You, but instead draw them to You. If I've bullied someone, I pray that You would forgive me and help me make it up to that person. I ask that You would heal the broken heart I've caused. And if I've been bullied, help me forgive those who've hurt me—just like You've forgiven me. Amen.

POWER UP:

When you think of bullying, you may think of little kids on a playground getting pushed around by kids who've flunked second grade one too many times. But the truth is, bullying can occur at any age—just ask someone who has been threatened or made the object of ridicule. It's a painful, scary, dreadful thing.

If you are the bully, stop it and ask Jesus to show you how your actions affect the person you're tormenting. Then ask for forgiveness and become a friend instead of a bully.

If you've been bullied, then make the decision to forgive the bully. If the situation is still happening, then pray for God's wisdom to know how to handle it, and consider getting a school counselor or a parent involved. There's no reason for you to be continually threatened—either physically, emotionally, or socially. Ask God to show you how to settle it.

BACKPEDALING

Bragging

 DOWNLOAD:

Don't call attention to yourself; let others do that for you.

Proverbs 27:2

"Ian, your mom and I have discussed it, and we think it would be a good idea to get you a car when you turn sixteen."

Ian couldn't believe his ears. His parents were going to buy him a car for his sixteenth birthday, which was only three months away. "Dad, that's awesome!"

"Yeah, it would sure help out for you to be able to drive yourself to school and to help take your brother and sister to their practices," his father reasoned.

"Sure, Dad. I can do that. What kind of car?" Ian asked, the enthusiasm evident in his voice.

His dad shrugged. "I don't know; something nice."

Ian was on cloud nine. He wanted a car, but he didn't think it would happen without making a really strong case to his parents. But now, it was their idea.

The next day at school, he approached his group of friends and loudly announced, "Hey, my parents are getting me a car for my sixteenth birthday." Everyone congratulated him.

"That is so cool, man. What kind of car?" his friend Derrick asked.

Ian smiled and slowly nodded, "My dad said it would be nice." Both of his parents drove really nice cars. His mother drove a company car, a Cadillac, which she exchanged every two years; and his dad drove a brand-new SUV. So he was sure that when his father said "nice," he meant new and loaded.

"You are so lucky," Derrick said with obvious envy in his voice. "I want a car, but my parents have said I have to buy one with my own money and pay for the insurance and the gas for it. I've been working, trying to raise the down payment, but I'm still a good six months away. And I turned sixteen five months ago."

Ian slapped Derrick's back. "Well, some of us are just lucky, I guess," he said with obvious pleasure. He couldn't help feeling pleased that he was the object of envy.

Not that it was unusual for Ian to be considered cool. He knew his family was well-off. They lived in an upscale neighborhood, and both of his parents had good jobs; he dressed well too. Girls had told him he was good-looking, and he was an above-average soccer player on his team. So life was pretty good. But with the right car, life would *rock*. He just knew it.

Over the next several weeks, he dreamed about the nice car he was going to get. Would it be a convertible? Would it have a kickin' sound system? Leather? Multiple CD changer? Ian scanned the latest issues of *Motor Trend* magazine, trying to decide on the perfect car. He began to research the latest road tests to find out which cars went from zero to seventy-five in the shortest amount of time. He studied which cars had the best reliability and fewest recalls. He wasn't into street racing, so he didn't need one to be that loaded, but it would be nice if it were tough.

"So do you know what car your parents are going to get you yet?" Derrick asked him one day before classes started.

"No, my dad said he'd find me a nice one. That's all I know," Ian said with confidence, "but I've got my eye on an Acura RSX or a Mustang GT."

"Are you kidding? Those are awesome cars. You really think you're going to get something like that?" Derrick asked in amazement.

Ian shrugged, looking cool and unimpressed. "Sure, why not? They're only twenty thou' or so."

Derrick's eyes grew the size of saucers. "Man, you are *so* lucky!"

Ian nodded as if to say, "Yeah, I know."

By the end of the week, the rumors about Ian's car flooded the school. Everyone was buzzing about it. Daily, students asked what car his parents were getting him and when they could see it. Ian noticed that he was even getting more attention from some of the girls who made him promise to take them for a ride.

Ian usually winked and teased, "I'll think about it."

A week before his birthday, his father announced, "Well, Ian, I found your car."

Ian was in the middle of swallowing a fork-full of meatloaf when his father's announcement almost caused him to choke. "Really?" he squeaked out.

"Yup, my coworker's wife is selling her car. I test drove it yesterday during lunch. I think you're going to like it," his dad said.

Ian frowned. "Your coworker's wife?"

"Uh-huh. It's a nice little 1996 Ford Escort. It'll work well for what you'll use it for."

Ian sat stunned and speechless. His mind couldn't even get around a used Ford Escort. "But Dad," he stuttered, "I thought you said my car would be nice."

His father stopped eating and looked at him with surprise. Then glancing toward Ian's mother, he looked back at Ian. "It *is* a nice car. It's in good condition—inside and out. It gets good gas mileage, so it won't be expensive for you. We can buy it outright, so you won't have to make any payments. I'd call that *very* nice."

Ian stared down at his food, thinking about all the planning he'd done over the last three months. He'd researched for the best "nice" car he could find, and now his parents were going to give him an old, used car. *What will my friends think?* he wondered, horrified. A queasy feeling slowly washed over him as he thought about all the kids at school. He'd told everyone he was getting something like a Acura RSX or a Mustang GT. Now, he'd have to eat his words. *How embarrassing!*

Through the rest of dinner, Ian sat quietly, trying to finish his food. Since it was Ian's night to clean up, he cleared the table, loaded the dishwasher, and prepared to hand wash some of the pots and pans. He couldn't stop thinking about the car.

"Ian, what kind of car did you think we were going to buy for you?" his father asked as Ian rinsed off the plates before putting them into the dishwasher.

"I don't know," Ian shrugged. "When you said 'nice' I thought you meant new."

"Don't you want the car?" his dad asked.

"Yes, I want it," Ian said, quickly backpedaling. "I just have to get used to the idea of a used car." Though he wasn't thrilled with the idea of a used car, especially one so common, he wasn't prepared to go without any car at all. Obviously, a used car—even a plain one—was better than no car.

The next day at school, Derrick approached Ian. "So next week is it."

Ian fidgeted uncomfortably. "Uh-huh."

"So any idea about what you're getting—the Acura RSX or a Mustang GT?" Derrick asked excitedly.

"Well," Ian said lamely, "I think my parents decided to get me something a little more practical."

Derrick frowned. "Practical?"

"Yeah, I think they want something less expensive like a Ford Escort," Ian offered.

Derrick started to chuckle. Then his chuckling turned to laughter. "You're kidding, right?" When Ian didn't answer, Derrick laughed even harder. "You've been telling everyone that you're getting a new Acura RSX or Mustang GT, and instead you're getting a used Ford Escort? What year?"

 **TRUTH UNPLUGGED:**

When good things happen to you, thank God for them instead of boasting about how great you are.

"1996."

More hysterical laughter.

Ian knew he deserved this, and he knew it was only the beginning. *Why did I have to shoot my mouth off?* he wondered. He knew that by the end of the day, he would be the laughingstock of the entire school. Of course, he should feel happy that he was getting *any* car, and a Ford Escort was a fine car; he knew that. But he'd let his imagination and mouth run away with him. Now, he was going to pay for it—dearly.

By the time he finally received his car, he'd already endured a week of being the butt of every joke. But when he got behind the wheel, he didn't care. He knew he'd be more cautious about bragging in the future. For now, he was going to enjoy his new, used car.

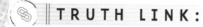

TRUTH LINK:

Dear Lord, help me to be careful with my words and not brag about my successes or boast about the things I receive. I know that anything good in my life comes from You, so help me to be humble and keep my mouth in check. Amen.

POWER UP:

Surely you've been around someone who brags. The person uses the good things that he or she receives—like a car—and the good things that happen to him or her to feel superior to others. You know it's hard to be around someone like that. Of course, becoming a braggart can be tempting. You have to be cautious not to become one. That doesn't mean you should lie about your successes or about the good things you receive, but it helps to maintain a thankful heart and a humble attitude. Give God thanks for those things and share them with others rather than using them to feel superior.

TRUTH IN THE FOG

Masturbation

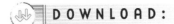 **DOWNLOAD:**

Just as you used to offer the parts of your body in slavery to impurity and to ever-increasing wickedness, so now offer them in slavery to righteousness leading to holiness. Romans 6:19 NIV

Clint's eyes watered as he stared at himself, a blurry reflection in his foggy bathroom mirror. His head dropped as he pulled a towel around his waist and leaned back against the wall. The surface cooled his heated skin.

He had done it again—this was the fifth time now—and his desire was growing. He hadn't expected that.

The first time he had done it, it was out of curiosity. The characters on his favorite TV show, *Jake's River,* talked about it flippantly, like masturbation was something every teenager did—*no— had* to do, to stay sexually satisfied.

So Clint tried it. And it scared him.

It was pleasurable—kind of. But it wasn't the "be-all and end-all" that the *Jake's River* bunch made it out to be. Still, the emotions were—unexpected.

Clint hadn't counted on the sudden, deep-seated guilt that followed. The first time it had happened was before school, and he could barely concentrate that day. His thoughts slipped back to the guilt he felt, like he was dirty, like he had done something terribly wrong. But eventually, the guilt lessened.

The second time he had done it, it was by choice.

It wasn't as pleasurable the second time, but more of a release. A brief escape from the troubles in his household. For a brief moment, he forgot about his nagging mother, his never-there father, and his annoying sister. The pleasure was brief, and suddenly, the guilt returned, flooding over him like a tidal wave.

He vowed never to do it again, no matter what. It was like a bad drug—pleasure for a moment, guilt for an eternity. A couple of days later, like a drug addict, he wanted to do it again. He wanted to escape. The guilt and shame returned.

Weeks had passed, and Clint found himself staring into his fogged-up bathroom mirror, wondering why he had ever started it at all. Because even though he vowed each time that it would be the last time, it never was. And the guilt actually increased, along with the need to do it *again*. Unfortunately, the guilt was stronger than the pleasure, yet his mind somehow blocked out that little fact until he had finished.

Clint's mind drifted to the times his pastor talked about guilt. Not that Clint was in the habit of listening much to his pastor—the *Jake's River* bunch certainly seemed to know more about life than *he* did. Still, they rarely talked about guilt on that show—and his pastor seemed to bring it up more frequently now that Clint was experiencing it nearly 24/7.

"When you do something wrong," he recalled his pastor's words, "your conscience will be your guide. You'll feel guilt—and that's the Holy Spirit letting you know that what you're doing is wrong." Then he said, "Keep doing wrong, and God will keep telling you to stop—it's a danger sign for your soul. If you refuse God's warnings and continue in the opposite direction, you'll begin to hear His voice less and less, and the guilt will go away as your heart hardens and a gulf forms between you and God."

Clint couldn't remember much more of the pastor's message. He and his friends had been whispering about a new girl on the second row that night, so the rest of the sermon was a blur.

Clint hated to admit it, but he thought his youth pastor might have had a point. The guilt did make him feel distant from God. Like he was in a boat, rowing in the opposite direction. He knew that all he had to do was stop rowing and turn around—but that was easier said than done. The current was strong.

 TRUTH UNPLUGGED:

When you feel guilty, realize it isn't God pressing down on you in anger. It's a gentle nudge, reminding you that not only does He want you to stay close to Him, but He also wants you to know that He's there to help you when you need it.

But what was so wrong with it anyway? It was natural, right? A natural part of life? Something *every* kid did at some time.

But Clint couldn't convince himself. And then he wondered, *Even if everyone else does do it, does that make it right for me? How can it be right if I feel so dirty?*

Bam! Bam! Bam! Clint jumped at the sound of the knocking on the door.

His sister shouted, "Get out, Clint! It's my turn!"

Suddenly, impulsively, Clint shouted back with a deep resonance in his voice that he had never used with his sister, "Shut up, idiot! I can take as long as I want!"

Not his words, but the tone must have pierced his sister, because he heard her whimper something softly and leave without arguing.

Clint looked up at the foggy mirror again. He could barely see his eyes staring back at him, wondering where that outburst had come from—though he already knew. It was the sound of a young man caught in his guilt—embarrassed, confused, and angry. He didn't like that sound.

"God, help me," he whispered, still staring at the mirror. Suddenly, he saw himself clearly—no mist, no fog—it was just he standing there, exposed. He saw that he wasn't a boy, but a man— a weak man, nothing more than flesh hanging on bone, with empty eyes staring back at him.

"I *do* need help, God," he whispered into the air. And though it was nothing he could grab onto with his physical hands, Clint knew the help was there—it had been all along. The guilt he felt was there to *help* him, only it wasn't guilt, but conviction—God calling on him, asking if He could *help* him stop using this drug because He didn't want Clint rowing away from Him. He wanted them to move in the same direction.

And at that moment, Clint made a firm decision. He grabbed the oars of his life and began paddling in the other direction with them. It didn't matter how hard the current flowed or how many people were going in the other direction. Clint was going to do what was right in his heart, what was pure, and what made him more than just weak flesh hanging on bone. He was going to do what would make him stronger. And he wasn't going to do it alone.

TRUTH LINK:

Dear Lord, more than anything, I want to be close to You. I don't want to do **ANYTHING** that would pull me away from You or make me sail in another direction—not even masturbation. Help me today—to live right and to listen—even to Your whispers. Amen.

POWER UP:

Television, movies, and locker-room talk try to convince you that sexual acts, such as masturbation, don't hurt anyone and are a natural part of growing up. But God says otherwise. God wants you to stay holy and pure before Him, not so you miss out on life, but because He wants you to have the most full life possible. God wants your life to be an adventure, side by side with Him, one that keeps all sexual activity safe within the boundaries of marriage. He hasn't left you to figure out how to do that on our own. No, He's there to help you stay holy, pure, and safe every day.

BUT I DIDN'T MEAN TO . . .

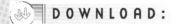

Responsibility

DOWNLOAD:

May integrity and uprightness protect me, because my hope is in you. Psalm 25:21 NIV

Ron held the cartons of eggs in his lap while Ethan drove slowly through the dark neighborhood. They'd planned this night for days. It was tradition. As players on the football team, they reveled in playing pranks on each other. And tonight was Preston Thompson's turn.

Preston had left Ethan with a welt the size of a silver dollar on his leg from a wet-towel snap in the locker room after the last game. Ethan promised to get him back. It was all just good-natured fun.

When Ron and Ethan arrived, they each grabbed a carton of eggs and sneaked up to Preston's lawn. Then taking aim, they began throwing the eggs at Preston's house, trying to stifle their laughter as they went.

From practice, they'd developed pretty good aim, so they were good at targeting the brick so as to muffle the sound of the eggs hitting the house. Slowly eggs splattered the house, leaving behind an oozy mess flecked with white eggshell.

Just when they were ready to leave, Ethan took his last egg and aimed at a window on the front of the house. Ron knew they shouldn't aim for windows, but before he could say anything, Ethan launched the final egg. Instead of hearing a thud, they heard the shattering of glass.

Ron and Ethan froze.

Looking at each other, Ethan yelled, "Let's get outta here."

Ron panicked as he ran toward Ethan's car and jumped in. Quickly, they sped away.

"Oh man, we're toast," Ron said trembling. "Why'd you aim for the window anyway?"

"I didn't mean to break it. I just wanted them to hear the final hit, so they'd come out and see it. I thought it'd be funny," Ethan reasoned.

Later that night when Ron entered his house, he found his dad sitting in the living room with a police officer. Ron felt his knees go weak.

"Ron, can you come in here?" his dad asked. Ron entered and had a seat on the sofa. "Where have you been tonight?"

Ron's mind raced. He knew better than to lie to his dad, but he also didn't want to get in trouble. "I was out with Ethan," he answered slowly.

Ron's dad looked at the officer, who cleared his throat before speaking. "It seems that there was a mishap at a house on Elm Street. It's the home of Larry Thompson and his family. Some kids egged his house, and one of the eggs hit a window and broke it. Do you know anything about that?"

"Yeah," Ron said slowly, nodding his head as he spoke. "It was an accident." The officer motioned for him to continue as he began to write in his small notebook. "It was just for fun. We're all on the football team, and we play jokes on each other. Ethan threw the last egg, and it hit the window. He didn't mean to break it."

As he spoke, the police officer continued writing. Nodding, the officer finally said, "I figured it was something like that. Mr. Thompson saw Ethan Mallory's car as he drove away. Preston said you were probably in on it too. Luckily, Mr. Thompson doesn't want to press any charges. He just wants the window replaced."

The officer continued talking to Ron's dad and making notes in his notebook. Ron didn't hear much of what was said. He was too relieved that Preston's dad wasn't going to press charges for the broken window.

When the officer left, Ron's dad returned to the living room. "Ron, that was a stupid stunt you pulled tonight."

"I know, Dad. Trust me, Ethan didn't mean to break the window."

"I'm not just talking about Ethan. You were there too. You're responsible too," his dad said with finality.

Confused, Ron reasoned, "But Dad, I didn't break the window."

His dad shook his head. "It doesn't matter. It's just like a football team. Although one guy may make or miss a touchdown, the whole team partakes in the victory or loss. You and Ethan went over there to egg Preston's house, so you're both responsible for whatever happened while you were there. You need to help pay for that window."

The next day before practice, Ron entered the locker room, wondering what kind of reception he'd get. "Hey, Preston," he said, "sorry about last night."

Preston turned to him. "Yeah, my dad was pretty hot at first, but he calmed down when I told him it was just a prank. He called the police before I could stop him, but I convinced him not to press charges. I told him about some of the pranks I've played on people, and he eased up."

Ron nodded.

Then Ethan walked into the locker room and came toward them. He apologized to Preston too. "I didn't mean to break the window. I just wanted you to hear it inside. I didn't think I threw it hard enough to break anything." The three of them made their peace, changed, and went outside for practice.

After practice when Ron and Ethan were walking out of the locker room, Ron turned to Ethan and said, "My dad says I have to pay for half of the window."

Ethan looked at him. "Really?"

"Yeah," Rob shrugged, "he said that even though you threw it, I was still there, a partner-in-crime kinda thing. He said I'm still responsible."

 **TRUTH UNPLUGGED:**

Taking responsibility for your actions isn't always easy, but with God's help, you can make it through challenging situations with integrity.

"What do *you* think?" Ethan asked, eyeing him cautiously.

"At first I didn't think so, but now I see his point," Rob said, nodding. "If I hadn't gone, you wouldn't have gone, and Preston's window wouldn't have been broken. So yeah, I'm partly responsible." Ethan didn't respond; instead he trudged silently beside Ron as he spoke. "I'm also grounded until I finish paying for my half. I can go to school, practice, and church; that's it."

Ethan smiled. "Me too."

Ron continued, "I guess my dad is going to call your mom and Preston's dad today and get everything squared away. So much for our fun prank, huh?"

"Yeah," Ethan laughed, "so much for that."

Ron spent the next two weeks doing odd jobs around the house for his dad in order to work off his debt. He wasn't thrilled with the outcome, but he was relieved that his punishment had only come from his dad and not the police. The more he thought about it, the more he realized that his dad was right. He was partly responsible for the broken window. It took him awhile to be able to look at an egg again, but he'd learned a lesson he wouldn't soon forget.

TRUTH LINK:

Dear Lord, help me to take responsibility for my actions, even when I find it difficult. I want to be a person of integrity, who doesn't run from trouble, but faces it, knowing that You are with me. Amen.

POWER UP:

Taking responsibility for your actions isn't always easy. Sometimes you can try to reason it away, saying that you didn't mean for something to happen or that you weren't directly responsible.

Part of becoming a person whom God can trust to do His work is facing challenging, uncomfortable situations. It doesn't mean that everything will always work out perfectly, but it does mean that He'll be there to help you face it. You won't be alone, and when you've put the situation behind you, you'll be able to stand proud, knowing you handled it with courage and integrity.

A WORLD OF DIFFERENCE

Salvation

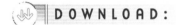
Adam woke up feeling as sluggish as he had every other day for as long as he could remember. He fought to open his eyes when his alarm clock screamed at him. Rolling out of bed, he stumbled to the bathroom. He haphazardly combed his hair, brushed his teeth, and splashed water on his face. It was the least he could do.

"Could you try not to look like you just rolled out of bed? If you'd just try a little, you could be a very handsome young man," his mother had often said. The problem was that Adam didn't want to try. Trying required too much effort, and he just couldn't be bothered.

Back in his room, he opened his closet to pull out clothes. It wasn't as if he really had to try to find clothes that matched. Everything he had was either black or gray. Occasionally, he mixed in a white T-shirt that had splashes of red or orange on it, but that was it. He knew other kids in school dressed in the latest clothes, but Adam couldn't bring himself to do it. He wouldn't be caught dead in something that looked like it came from an uppity store at the mall. Plus, the darker he looked, the fewer people got in his way. With all the school shootings and other craziness, kids steered clear of the dark, scary people. Not that Adam was on the verge of a shooting rampage or anything. No, he just preferred jeans and T-shirts, and if he could find them both in black, so much the better.

Down in the kitchen, he fixed himself a bowl of oatmeal.

"What's your day going to be like?" his mother asked cheerfully.

Adam hated these conversations; he had nothing to add. "I don't know. School, I guess," he said with a shrug. It wasn't that he was trying to be difficult or sullen; he just didn't know what else to say. Life was life, and his was what it was.

"Honestly Adam, you make it sound like you have it so tough," his mother said with irritation. "You know, you have it pretty good."

Adam knew that without much provocation, he and his mother could be in a huge fight in a matter of seconds, so he didn't answer and went on eating his cereal.

He and his mother used to be close, but since his parents' divorce, they'd drifted apart. Adam didn't really feel sad about the divorce. Sometimes he felt angry, but mostly he didn't feel anything. He knew his parents had been unhappy for years, but he'd always hoped they'd work things out. Then one day, they'd made the announcement that they were separating. Six months later, their divorce became final, and six months after that, his dad had taken a job out of state. Now, Adam only saw him on select holidays and during the summer.

Adam supposed things had been okay since then. His mother worked long hours, so they didn't see each other much. The only time they had together was in the mornings over breakfast, and unfortunately for both of them, Adam wasn't a morning person. He didn't like to talk before 10 A.M. So they were left communicating through grunts in the morning and notes on the table at night.

At school, Adam drifted from class to class. He just couldn't get excited about school. He had been an A-B student, but that was back in the days when he cared about school. Now, he found the classes boring and the other students obnoxious. He made decent grades when he tried, but without trying, he could skate by with a solid C. That was good enough for him.

Lunchtime at his school had its own life. While the other students broke up into groups and noisily chatted away the hour, Adam usually bought a sandwich and drifted out to the portable classrooms to sit on the steps. Sometimes someone stopped to say hello, but most of the time he ate alone. He really didn't want to be around people; he just wanted to be left alone.

"Hey, Adam," Josh Lipton called. Josh was a guy in Adam's art class. He always wore T-shirts that said things like "Jesus Rocks" or "Heaven-Bound." Today was no different.

Whatever floats your boat, Adam thought.

"I was wondering if you'd like to come to a party with me?" Josh asked.

Adam almost turned around to see if Josh was talking to someone behind him. *Surely, he can't be talking to me.* "What kind of party?" he asked hesitantly.

"It's at a friend's house. We're going to play games and eat pizza. It'll be fun."

"Okay," Adam said before he could stop himself. After Josh had given him all the specifics—date, time, place—and left, Adam wanted to slap himself. *Why did I say I'd go?* He had no idea.

On the night of the party, Adam arrived a few minutes late. He would have called to cancel but realized he didn't have Josh's phone number. *I guess I don't have a choice,* he thought.

At the party, he looked around and realized that he didn't know most of the people there. Some looked vaguely familiar, but most were complete strangers. Adam stood on the fringe, waiting for enough time to pass so he could leave without being rude.

"Adam, come join us," Josh called from a group playing Ping-Pong. "It's so cool that you came." Watching his reaction, Adam realized that Josh really was glad to see him, even though for the life of him he couldn't understand why. Most people didn't even notice him. Adam had worked so hard to disappear that he was surprised when someone actually saw him.

After playing games for a while, everyone congregated in the living room. Adam realized after he arrived that this was Josh's church group. "Okay, listen up, everyone," a guy who was probably in his late twenties called, "Let's bless the pizza, so we can dig in.

"Dear Lord, we're here tonight to have a great time and enjoy each other's company. I pray that You would bless this food and our time together. I also pray that You would help any new people have a good time and feel comfortable. In Jesus' name we pray. Amen," he said, and everyone gave him a hearty amen in response.

After dinner, people continued to talk. Adam sat on the floor in the living room watching everyone like they were characters on a television show. They seemed to be really nice to each other in a brother-sister kind of way.

"Hey Adam, you having fun?" Josh asked as he sat down next to him on the floor.

"Yeah, it's a fun group," Adam responded. After a few seconds of silence, he asked, "Josh, why did you invite me?"

Josh smiled. "I don't know. I was praying, and I asked God whom I should invite; and your face came to my mind. I kind of took it as a sign."

Adam didn't know how to respond, so he sat quietly for a few more seconds. "So do you pray often?" he finally asked.

"Yeah, I do. I talk to God about my day and what I'm thinking about and what I'm worried about and how I'm feeling about things. Stuff like that."

"And you think He hears you?" Adam asked puzzled.

Josh laughed. "Well, you're here, aren't you? I mean if I hadn't prayed, then God wouldn't have made me think of you, and you wouldn't have accepted. So yeah, I think He hears me."

"That must be nice," Adam said looking away. "I mean, it must be nice to have someone who listens to you whenever you have something to say."

"You know you can talk to Him too," Josh said.

Adam smiled and nodded as if he knew that, but inside he wondered if God really would listen to him. Would He hear his prayers? Could he tell Him everything that went through his mind and everything he felt?

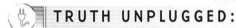 **TRUTH UNPLUGGED:**

You will find no greater purpose, meaning, or fulfillment in life than that which you find in Jesus.

Later that night, Adam lay in bed thinking about what Josh had said. In desperation, he closed his eyes and whispered, "God, I don't know if You can hear me or even if You care, but I'd really like to know if You're there. I don't like my life the way it is, but I don't know how to change it. Can You help?" He waited to hear an audible answer. When he didn't, he rolled over and closed his eyes. *Oh well,* he thought, *it was worth a shot.*

During lunch the following Monday, Adam took his regular spot on the portable's steps to eat his sandwich. A few minutes after he arrived, Josh joined him. "Hey Adam."

"Oh hi, Josh. Thanks again for inviting me to your party," he said.

"No problem. I'm glad you came," Josh answered. Then shifting uncomfortably from foot to foot, Josh said, "Listen Adam, I was praying this weekend, and I kept seeing your face in my mind. I felt like God wanted me to tell you something." Adam silently watched him. "I felt like He wanted you to know that He loves you and He sees you. And He knows you're not happy with your life the way it is, and He wants to help."

Adam felt the blood drain from his face. Josh had answered the exact questions Adam had prayed.

Josh quickly sat down beside him, "Are you okay?"

Adam explained that he had prayed to God about the exact things Josh had just said.

Josh laughed and slapped his back. "That's awesome!" he exclaimed.

"What do I do now?" Adam asked in desperation.

Josh smiled. "You pray and ask Jesus into your heart." When Adam looked at him in confusion, Josh said, "Just repeat what I pray: Dear Lord, I know that I need You in my life, and not only do I need You, but I want You in my life. I pray that You would forgive me for my sins. I realize that Jesus is the Son of God, and I dedicate my life to serving You. Please show me what to do now. Amen."

Adam repeated the prayer as Josh said it. When he finished, he opened his eyes. He didn't know what to expect. Would there be lightning bolts? Would he hear an audible voice *now?* Instead, he heard Josh exclaim, "This is so cool!"

As the weeks went by, Adam felt as though the dark cloud he had lived under had left. Things didn't change immediately, but as he continued to pray and read the Bible, he began to feel hopeful about life. He began to attend church with Josh, and eventually, his mother joined him. He met new friends from the youth group and began to see a much bigger plan for his life. While only weeks prior he'd found it impossible to see good in anything, now he saw possibilities everywhere. He'd allowed God's unmistakable presence to come into his life, and it had made a world of difference.

TRUTH LINK:

Dear Lord, I believe that Jesus is the Son of God and that He died on the cross for me. I ask for Your forgiveness for my sins. I want to dedicate my life to serving You. Please help me to live the Christian life and to find Christian friends. Thank You for coming into my life. Amen.

POWER UP:

As you've read the devotions in this book, have you realized that something is missing in your life? Have you tried to find meaning in other ways, only to continue to feel a void in your life?

Every single person in the world is meant to have a relationship with Jesus. Each of us decides whether to allow Him into our lives or not, but if you do, you'll find more meaning and fulfillment in life—pure and simple. He is always there waiting to listen to you, help you, and direct you. There is no greater journey you will ever take than the one you take with Jesus. Don't wait—He wants to be a part of your life today.

And if you've given your life to Jesus in the past, but have fallen away from Him, it's okay. He still loves you. In fact, He never stopped. No matter what you've done, you're never beyond His love. Make the decision to rededicate your life to Him. Then find a church or a Christian club at school where you can make solid, Christian friends.

Get ready—you've just begun the adventure of your life! And that's the Truth—unplugged.

TOPICAL INDEX

Anger 20

Attitude 146

Bragging................231

Bullying 225

Church...................82

Criticism 172

Death 189

Decision-making 73

Difficult Parents......135

Divorce 15

Drugs 30

Drinking 36

Diligence 42

Encouragement.......130

Faithfulness 156

Family Changes..........25

Fantasy 124

Forgiveness.............68

Giving 113

Holy Spirit 220

Honor...................103

Illness 167

Inner Strength..........99

Jealousy.................94

Joy 47

Love 78

Lying 204

Masturbation 237

Materialism 210

Mentoring 9

Patience...............194

Peace 62

Persecution 151

Pornography 141

Prayer 108

Pride....................51

Profanity 183

Racism 215

Rejection 57

Responsibility.........242

Salvation 247

Sex 118

Sibling Rivalry.........161

Suicide 199

Trusting God 88

Thankfulness 177